D0273042

Online Marketing to Investors

How to Develop Effective Investor Relations

Daniel Valentine
University of Oxford

BUSINESS EXPERT PRESS

Online Marketing to Investors: How to Develop Effective Investor Relations

Copyright © Business Expert Press, LLC, 2015.

All rights reserved. No part of this publication may be reproduced, stored in a retrieval system, or transmitted in any form or by any means—electronic, mechanical, photocopy, recording, or any other except for brief quotations, not to exceed 400 words, without the prior permission of the publisher.

First published in 2015 by
Business Expert Press, LLC
222 East 46th Street, New York, NY 10017
www.businessexpertpress.com

ISBN-13: 978-1-63157-140-4 (paperback)
ISBN-13: 978-1-63157-141-1 (e-book)

Business Expert Press Finance and Financial Management Collection

Collection ISSN: 2331-0049 (print)
Collection ISSN: 2331-0057 (electronic)

Cover and interior design by S4Carlisle Publishing Services Private Ltd., Chennai, India

First edition: 2015

10 9 8 7 6 5 4 3 2 1

Printed in the United States of America.

Online Marketing
to Investors

Abstract

This book introduces the online marketing and disclosure techniques which enable listed corporations to engage effectively with financial markets. These techniques are part of the discipline of Investor Relations (IR) which is the corporate function responsible for advising the senior officers of a listed company on the relationship between the company and the market for corporate stock. As a corporate function, IR is very young in the United Kingdom, but since the 1980s, it has rapidly penetrated the highest levels of corporate management as its value becomes clearer. The marketing of corporate stock is a key part of the value of effective IR, although the highly regulated nature of the world's leading stock markets means that a specialized form of marketing is required.

Digital channels present great but underutilized potential to contribute to ever more effective IR. Online platforms offer fast, comprehensive, economical, flexible, and regulation-compliant methods of disclosing corporate information to investors, analysts, and other relevant parties in the investment evaluation and decision-making process. This book examines the ways in which digital mechanisms can facilitate the building of transparent, mutually-beneficial, and lasting relationships between companies and the investors and financial analysts that comprise the U.K. equity markets, using both established and emerging channels and technology, within the constraints of the U.K. regulatory context and customs of the equity markets. The problems with using "social media" in particular for disclosure are discussed, and a number of risks connected with use of the new media are explored. The book concludes by summarizing the key challenges facing investor marketing in the next decade.

Keywords

Investor Marketing, Financial Public Relations, Investor Relations, Corporate Communications, Shareholders, Public Relations, Corporate Governance, Finance

Advanced Quotes for Online Marketing to Investors

Investor relations is no dark art, but an essential, and strategic, communications function. This book is full of excellent advice, and will change the way you engage with investors. Every CEO, CFO and Communications Director should buy it.

Francis Ingham
Director General of the Public Relations Consultants
Association (PRCA) & Executive Director of the International
Communications Consultancy Organisation (ICCO)

In this accessible and well-written book, Daniel Valentine provides a helpful primer on the terms of reference for investor relations activities. His analysis of the role of social media in communicating the investment case is both timely and relevant.

Alex Money
Managing Director of ACE Consensus
University of Oxford

This book clearly explains why Investor Relations is now a highly regarded career choice and demonstrates its value to companies and the investment community.

Helen Parris
Director of Investor Relations
G4S plc

This book is an essential read for Investor Relations professionals, business managers, and anyone interested in corporate relations.

William Sun
Deputy Director of the Centre for Governance
Leadership and Global Responsibility
Leeds Business School

Contents

List of Figures

Preface

The last few years have seen some of the United Kingdom's largest companies get into serious difficulties because of their failure to communicate effectively with the financial markets. Some companies were engaged in a deliberate attempt to mislead; others were guilty of negligence and ignorance.

The crisis that hit Tesco plc in September 2014, and is still being played out as this book is being published, demonstrates the need for listed companies to regularly update both their own forecasts and market expectations. Communication is not enough, however. Tesco misunderstood its own customers and grossly underestimated the ambition and ability of two relatively small competitors who quickly seized the opportunity presented by changing customer values. The Tesco debacle illustrates the two aspects of IR: the communication aspect and the analytical aspect. IR (like public relations) is not just a communication function, but also an analytical function. IR helps management to understand its own environment, and then conveys that understanding to the financial markets. Endless books on "communication" get this wrong because they suggest that communication is virtuous in itself, and that most problems are simply communication problems. IR does not just **communicate** the performance of the firm; it **facilitates** the performance of the firm by providing the management team with both the analysis of the financial markets and its own analysis, based on a deep knowledge of the firm, its products, investors, customers, and competitors. IR has great potential to contribute to corporate success, investor wealth, and society at large. The study of IR, however, poses significant challenges. IR is a complex, discrete and highly context-dependent activity, which takes a different form in every corporation in which it is practiced. The paucity of IR-related books is not surprising, but is a major obstacle to the development of IR as a profession and as a field of study.

This book presents a methodology for investor marketing which is the product of both wide research and personal experience. This book aims to provide IROs (investor relations officers) with ideas and principles of action, but no book on IR can provide the steps that the reader needs to take at the moment of reading; the work of the IR practitioner is far too diverse for any formulaic guidance. The good IRO has to base his or her actions on his or her own environment, and use good judgment sharpened by experience. If this book encourages readers to review their IR practices, then it will have served its purpose.

Daniel Valentine

Hertford College, University of Oxford

March 19, 2015

CHAPTER 1

The Purpose of Investor Relations

Financial markets serve an essential purpose in advanced economies. Like markets of every type, financial markets are mechanisms that facilitate mutual satisfaction through exchange. Behind exchange is the principle of specialization (or "division of labor"), the principle behind all economic growth. Economic growth thus relies on specialization, which in turn relies on the existence of a mechanism of exchange which is easily accessible and that market participants regard as fair, secure, and efficient.

This book will examine one particular financial market: the market for equities, or shares, of listed companies. Equity markets give access to almost limitless amounts of capital, allowing companies to grow rapidly. They also contain many traps for corporations and executives. This book has been written to help company executives, and their advisors, get things right the first time.

Equity markets' expectation levels for information have risen substantially over the last decade as investors and intermediaries have sought informational advantage. The last decade has presented extra opportunities and challenges for all financial market participants, including boards of directors, investors, analysts, and regulators. Investors have acquired new tools of data capture and analysis through the Internet, which has also presented companies with an unprecedented ability to engage directly and frequently with investors, both large and small, as well as with journalists, analysts, suppliers, customers, and other stakeholders. However, there are regulatory restrictions and reputational risks that public companies need to be aware of when communicating with financial markets, especially when using social media channels that give control to information users rather than senders.

Defining Investor Relations

Investor relations (IR) is a specialism that develops within listed corporations operating in advanced equity markets which have experienced a substantial separation of ownership and control. IR is a complex, discreet, and highly context-dependent discipline. It is therefore not a simple task to define IR in such a way that includes all typical tasks and excludes other financial and investor communication functions within the firm.

IR is the corporate function responsible for satisfying both the demands of regulators and the legitimate information needs of the financial markets beyond the financial statements and thereby facilitating mutually beneficial investment decisions and a harmonious relationship with the stock market.

Because of the failure of business schools and the accountancy profession to provide education in IR, new chief executive officers (CEOs) and chief financial officers (CFOs) are likely to receive a "culture shock" on their first appointments. In response to this shock, they may rely too heavily on external advisors from investment banks whose advice is less than impartial. It is the hope of the author that a better system of IR training is instituted so that mid-level executives are introduced to IR and can gather experience over a number of years before they reach board level. The work of IR professional bodies such as the National Investor Relations Institute (NIRI) in the United States, the Canadian Investor Relations Institute (CIRI) in Canada, and the IR Society in the United Kingdom is essential in this regard, although these institutes naturally tend to focus on IR professionals and consultants rather than accountants and general managers. If this book can make a contribution to the challenge of educating managers in the law and culture of the financial markets, then it will have served its purpose.

This book aims to contribute to the production of positive and mutually beneficial relationships between corporate managers and investment managers in order that these two interdependent groups benefit the ultimate beneficiaries: the general public, who rely on the employment, products, dividends, and pensions that corporations provide.

The Purpose of IR

IR emerged as a response to a series of shocks that hit corporate management teams from the mid-1970s. The autonomy of management was being challenged by investors who had shown they were able to directly control corporations. Many management teams that had resisted shareholder demands had been replaced. Management teams started to bring experienced city people in-house to advise them on investor sentiment and prevent investor threats. Mere information provision was no longer enough; management teams needed to form relationships with their largest investors and other opinion formers in the valuation and investment process.

IR is not independent; it is a department of the firm; and yet it derives much of its credibility with the investment community from its sympathy with investors. IR thus becomes an "insider" with both communities, and this dual credibility is the secret of IR success.

Figure 1.1 shows the three corporate goals of IR. These three goals are at the same time complementary and often in conflict. IR combines a sales function with a service function and a compliance function. The IR function provides important services to the financial community; it is also responsible for marketing the company within that community and ensuring

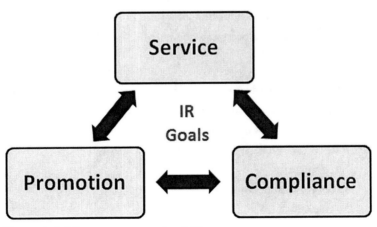

Figure 1.1 The corporate goals of IR

that the company does not breach any of the regulations relating to financial market communication. This makes the investor relations officer (IRO) simultaneously a police officer, a salesman, and an inquiry desk. It is this goal diversity of IR work that provides the IR function with much of its challenge, but also ensures a high corporate profile for the IRO.

IR as an Agent of Change

Ivy Lee (1877–1934) is credited with changing the practice of public relations (PR) from one which relied on propaganda-based persuasion to one that focused on the communication of understanding and mutual adjustment. The idea of mutual adjustment has been a feature of the most enlightened PR activities since then, and was defined as such by Lesly in the first edition of his influential handbook (1971): "Public relations helps an organization and its publics adapt mutually to each other." Likewise, IR at its best can promote communication and change in both directions: from shareholder to management as well as from management to shareholder. The company gains when management receives insight and warnings from investors, and the company also gains when investors develop in their understanding and sympathy for the company, its history, culture, position, and goals. The two parties engage in a continual process of mutual adjustment and find a greater area of common ground where their goals coincide.

The most specific benefit of this mutual adjustment is that management has regular access to informed criticism. The typical failings of corporate management have been well documented:[1]

- Excessive growth
- Margin deterioration
- Entering markets without clear competitive advantage
- Remaining in loss-making markets
- Diversification
- Hoarding cash
- Excessive remuneration and benefits
- Strategic drift
- Forecast optimism

---

[1]For instance by Lev, 2012, pp33-35 & Mckee, 2005, pp13-22.

- Earnings management
- Excessive charitable/political donations
- Risk aversion
- Preferring collusive agreements to effective rivalry
- Unjustified acquisitions

Investors play an important role in challenging management because of their analytical resource, industry-wide perspective, macroeconomic knowledge, and unique authority to request access to management. Management should therefore welcome the views of investors even when these views are critical. It is essential for corporate success that management teams learn of their own problems before their competitors do, and analysts and investors are a key resource in this respect.

The Relevance of Firm Size

Much of the discussion in this book presumes that communicating with sell-side analysts is a central part of the role of IR. This is true of large- and medium-cap companies, but much less true with small-cap companies, companies with a secondary listing and, companies listed on the Alternative Investment Market (AIM). Analysts have a strong preference for large-cap companies because of the potential commission revenue that this coverage may bring to their firm. While FTSE100 companies typically have in excess of 20 analysts, FTSE250 companies may just have two or three. The challenge for IR is thus very different in these two cases. Large companies will find they have to do very little "marketing"; their size alone will attract more suitors than they can meet, while small companies will have to market themselves in multiple ingenious ways to attract a flow of interested investors.

The IR requirements of a small-cap company are likely to be very different from the requirements of a large- or mega-cap company. The nature of analyst remuneration means that large companies are chased by a large (often excessive) number of analysts while mid-cap companies suffer comparative neglect and small-cap companies total neglect. Mega-cap companies may have in excess of 30 analysts; many of whom are largely regurgitating each other's work. Management of existing analysts

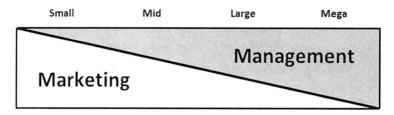

Figure 1.2 The IR marketing-management mix

and investors is a major challenge for large-cap companies, as shown in Figure 1.2. Management tasks include handling the steady stream of information requests, requests for meetings and requests for feedback on models, keeping track of analyst notes, and analyst consensus. Large-cap companies try to produce efficiencies with group-lunches for analysts and comprehensive "investor/analyst days" in order to reduce the pressure for one-on-one meetings. Protecting executive time is a major concern for larger companies, because of the sheer number of requests for meetings. At the other end of the scale, smaller companies require a constant marketing focus to attract the attention of analysts and institutional investors.

The Limits of IR

IR has a number of very serious limitations on its effectiveness. We list six of these below; each of which is common to all practitioners of PR:

1. The limited "voice" that IR has within the organization. IR typically reports to the CFO and has limited access to the CEO or board. IR thus has little influence on corporate strategy or performance. The ability of IR to produce corporate change remains limited, except in a shareholder crisis situation, when IR may have much greater power.

2. Investor heterogeneity. Changes that one investor requests may be resisted by another shareholder; shareholders show considerable diversity in their preference for corporate strategy, risk, or distribution of profits. So "getting close" to shareholders may not bring greater clarity of corporate goals or corporate strategy.

3. Intermediation. Much communication with investors is done indirectly, through analysts and journalists, and the messages that management want to communicate may not be transmitted or may be corrupted. Similarly, the messages that investors want to communicate to management may change as they pass through the hands of intermediaries.

4. The effect of IR activity is not capable of being rigorously measured. Difficulties in measuring IR contribute to its low profile and its low level of resourcing in the business.

5. IR's lack of independence from senior management.

6. IR's nature as an art, rather than a profession or science. The IRO is not a semiautonomous professional like an accountant or lawyer who follows long established work methods. Outside of the statutory aspects of IR, IR resembles PR or marketing in its highly opportunistic and adaptable nature. There is little even in the way of universal best practice. The IR activity at different firms varies hugely, and there is little evidence of convergence.

IR is a practice that can make great contributions despite these limits. Understanding these six limitations should help IROs play a credible and significant role in their corporations.

CHAPTER 2

The Development of Investor Relations

The term *investor relations* (IR) is a recent one, but many of the core tasks of IR have long histories. This book includes a history of IR because IR is a complex phenomenon that can only be understood historically and because no published history of IR currently exists.

Nine of the most significant influences behind the growth of IR since the mid-1970s are shown in Figure 2.1. It is worth analyzing these factors in detail since the origin of IR has not been well documented, and many of these trends are still in progress and continue to shape the practice of IR.

From the mid-1970s, the investor–corporation relationship became less passive from both sides. Investors became less tolerant of managerial

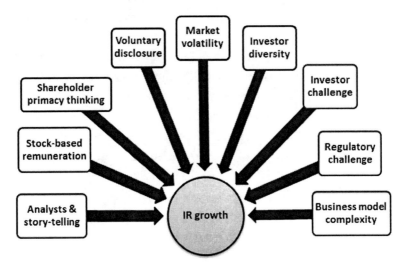

Figure 2.1 Nine key influences on the growth of IR

failure, and managers soon became more sensitive to investor expectations. Investors were also more inclined to closely monitor companies following increased pressure from clients and regulators. The techniques of IR were developed by management teams from the late 1970s as a defense mechanism against shareholder activism. These techniques became commonplace in the early 1980s.

The relationship between firms and investors changed substantially following the "Big Bang" deregulation of the London Stock Exchange in 1986. This introduced telephone and electronic trading and abolished the fixing of commissions, which quickly eroded the "old boy network" in the London markets. With the demise of local relationships came the rapid domination of foreign investment banks. Trading became much easier, and the U.S. model of financial analysts was introduced to assist investors make investment decisions. The internationalization of the London Stock Exchange after 1986 was one aspect of the **increasing diversity** of investors; another aspect was the growth of "ethical" investment which was promoted by the growth of public sector and religious bodies investing pension fund assets in ordinary stock, but providing their asset managers with mandates that included ethical rules. The wider availability of short selling put extra pressure on management teams. The emergence of "dark pools" (mechanisms where investors can trade stock secretly without declaring trades to the market) also reduced managerial visibility of stock movements. This required management to put extra emphasis on regular meetings with investors to gather feedback. The growth in **investor diversity**, also includes the growth of hedge funds, activist funds, ethical funds, and foreign investors. In classical abstract economic analysis, all shareholders have the same requirements. In fact this is far from the case. Investors are already diverse, and the trend is toward greater diversity.

Also in the 1980s, **increasing access to debt finance** (especially the emergence of high yield "junk" bonds) created a new breed of aggressive "corporate raiders" who started to challenge the large conglomerate corporations. The hostile takeover boom of the 1980s resulted in hundreds of firms in the United Kingdom and United States being purchased in leveraged buyouts; many of the targets then being asset stripped. The incumbent management teams were usually replaced, and new teams installed. The **increasing short-termism** and nervousness of investors created a growing disparity between the lengthening time frame applicable to most board-level decisions, and the reducing investment time frame of most professional investors.

Shareholder primacy thinking reemerged in the late 1970s generally dated from Milton Friedman's 1970 article, which was validated by Jenson & Mecking in 1976 and became mainstream in the 1980s. Several strands of this thinking emerged: in economics it emerged as "agency theory" (Jenson and Meckling, 1976; Fama 1980) and in investment it emerged as "shareholder value." It was soon endorsed by leading chief executive officers (CEOs) most notably by Jack Welch in 1981. (Deakin, 2010). "Shareholder value" asserts that management owes their loyalty exclusively to the task of maximizing the firm's value from a shareholder perspective, and the interests of other groups, if recognized at all, were to be subordinated to shareholder interests.

The popularity of **agency theory** was closely connected to the spread of performance-based pay, in the form of bonuses and stock options, as suggested by Jenson and Meckling in their 1976 article. Investors pressured remuneration committees into creating substantial stock-option packages for CEOs and chief financial officers (CFOs); tying managerial pay increases to stock market performance. The stock options succeeded in focusing the CEO and CFO on the stock price, but failed to align executives with shareholders. The fact that CEOs were being given the option to buy discounted shares with no danger of losing money made their position far different from that of investors (although quite similar to the position of fund managers who also enjoyed asymmetrical reward structures). Rather than resolving the agency problem, executive stock options merely pushed it one stage further along the investment chain.

The willingness of investors to engage with, and challenge, management has grown since the 1970s for a number of reasons. One reason is the **growth of activist investors**. There are different types of activists, from the "moral activist" who tend to be public pension funds to the short-term investors, especially hedge funds who are willing to influence analysts and journalists to pressure management to change policy. Certain U.S. pension funds, most notably CalPERS, have set the example of enforcing high standards of corporate governance and ESG policies, and this example has been followed to a more limited degree by public pension funds such as Hermes in the United Kingdom. Another reason is the **emergence of collective initiatives by investors** which has facilitated collective action. For instance, the International Corporate Governance Network (ICGN), which was initially founded by pension funds in 1995, has now more than 300 members—mainly fund managers. Another reason is **the growth of institutional ownership.** Since the 1960s, much of the diffusion of ownership that Berle and Means (1932) identified as the source of the governance problem has been reversed, with the decline of private investment as a proportion of the stock market. Institutional ownership now accounts for over 80 percent of U.K. equities, with the top 10 firms alone accounting for 25 percent of the market (Gaved, 1997). This concentration and the illiquidity it sometimes implies, together with increased competition between investors, have arguably given the investors both the opportunity and the need to actively manage their relationships with companies. (Roberts et al, 2011)

Although **analysts** had been around in the United States since the 1920s, with the first research department created in 1926 (Groysberg and Healy, 2013), the Wall Street crash depressed the nascent industry. A very gentlemanly form of competition developed with very constrained competition between analysts, who were well recompensed out of the substantial negotiated commissions that stockbrokers were paid for transactions. This cosy pattern was gradually ended by the Securities and Exchange Commission in a series of commission cuts during the early 1970s and then terminated by the abolition of negotiated commission on 1st May 1975. The sell-side analyst in the United States now returned to the 1920s model of aggressive selling of stock. This pattern had an influence on the United Kingdom from the late 1970s as U.S. investment banks looked to expand overseas due to the fierce competition in the United States, and the sleepy London Stock Exchange was a natural target. The late 1970s saw a growth in analyst research and investor aggression in the United Kingdom. The IR society was formed in 1980 in the middle of this turmoil, following the growth of IR. The investor relations officer (IRO) quickly became a key executive at many listed firms, tasked with managing this new relationship with analysts and investors. The 1980s saw the aggressive "shake-out" of many British industries who were rapidly exposed to foreign competitors following the ending of the formerly rigorous exchange controls in 1979. Analysts who were CFA or MBA trained brought a new language learned in U.S. business schools. Many British firms had been carefully managed with employee consent, because of the sensitive industrial relations atmosphere in the United Kingdom. U.S. analysts and investors were intolerant of trade unions and evolutionary change. They rapidly assessed corporate strategy, managerial talent, and market position. CEOs and CFOs were forced to learn this language quickly, and IROs were tasked with developing these corporate stories, writing the management "commentary" that became a required part of annual reports, and meeting with analysts to provide them with the background knowledge about the business that they needed to write their reports. Analyst reports now became a key weapon in the competition between investment banks for clients and trading commissions. Reports became more frequent and more aggressive. Analysts needed to change their story on a company several times a year to generate new waves of transactions, and so analysts became more journalistic in their search for "angles" and "stories" and more prone to hyperbole. Analysts began to draw on a wider range of data to create their stories and pressed management for more disclosure.

Business model complexity grew in the 1980s for a number of reasons. More managers and analysts were receiving business school training with the growth of the MBA and "Executive MBA" and the growing demand for financial qualifications, ACA and CFA being preferred. Managers were now able to implement the latest thinking, and the spread of ideas was facilitated by the growth in international business publishing. Asian, European, and American business ideas now found easy acceptance (encouraged by the increasingly international market for top executive talent). Peters and Waterman (1982) started a new trend, a business book that preached universal principles, had a research foundation, and used popular language. Airport lounge bookstores now become libraries disseminating business knowledge that could be digested within a two-hour plane trip. "Business models" became increasingly relevant to corporate success, with consultants offering corporate redesign involving contracting out, divisionalization, and downsizing. All business functions were now expected to offer flexibility, efficiency, strategic contribution and measurable value.

Distribution became "logistics," and HRM became "strategic HRM," as departments competed for professional status and a seat at the board table. The increasing complexity of business meant that analysts and investors spent more time analyzing firms and analyst reports became more like consultancy reports. IROs had to learn the latest concepts in strategy and management since analysts would compare firms against each other and highlight any firms that weren't adopting the latest thinking.

"**Voluntary disclosure**" became an important part of competing for capital in the 1970s and 1980s due to the growth of "intangible" value, the emergence of greater business model diversity, and the declining usefulness of financial statements for investment decision-making (Lev and Zarowin, 1999). This extra information imposed a double burden on firms; the information had to be not only collected and reported but analysts often required talking through the information by the firm, since much of the new disclosure was technical and industry specific. Since the 1970s, it has been commonplace to note the growing limitation of accounting information in firm valuation, due to the increasing importance of nonfinancial assets (Gazdar, 2007) such as reputation and human resources which explain the difference between book value and market value. The most extreme examples include firms like Apple, Microsoft, and Coca-Cola, whose verifiable assets may represent less than 10 percent of the market value of the firm. This leaves accountants struggling to account for the value of the firm, and other methods of evaluation have evolved to plug the gap between book value and market value.

Finally, growing **pressure from regulators,** including increased regulation of corporate decision-making after the creation of the Financial Reporting Council (FRC) in 1990 and the publication of the Cadbury Report in 1992, started the industry of "corporate governance" analysis. One of the most effective changes effected by regulators has been the crackdown on **"creative accounting" techniques** developed by corporations in the 1980s. Creative accounting has two aims: the inflation of profits, for short-term share price improvement, which must generally end in disaster, and the leveling of profits, known as "income smoothing," which is a way of making financial results less erratic then they would usually be to satisfy the market's unreasonable demand for ever increasing profits. Revenue and profit are given special status by the market as indicators of corporate well-being, far beyond their actual ability to represent this. Analysts and investors have unrealistic expectations about the predictability and stability of profit. Even small falls in profit for a period can result in a severe stock price penalty, since profit is used as a signal of corporate health. Because corporate executives are aware of the market's focus on profit and revenue, they go to great lengths to protect these figures from deterioration, involving complex accounting and budgeting procedures, the reclassification of assets and activities, and transfers between different corporate entities. Abraham J. Brilof, professor of accounting at the City University of New York, was an early critic of creative accounting and inept auditing, writing articles since the late 1960s, and publishing an influential book, *Unaccountable Accounting*, in 1972, and four years later publishing *The Truth About Corporate Accounting*. Much of what Brilof urged was finally accomplished in SOX. Terry Smith's famous book published in 1992 revealed the extent of the abuse of accounting standards, and initiated a response by the United Kingdom's FRC to make standards less flexible, as well as making analysts and investors more careful when reading financial statements. Since the scope for creative accounting began to reduce, the other way of managing expectations—"guidance"—became more important. The art of guidance is one of the key skills of the IRO, and so IR grows in importance as creative accounting has become more restricted, as accounting standards have become more precise, as investors have grown less tolerant of it, and as prosecuting authorities have become more vigorous. The growth of regulation alongside increasing penalties (both fines and stock price effects) for misconduct meant that a specialist compliance resource was needed, and IR took on this role.

This brief history has shown how modern IR is the product of a long period of development. Two things seem clear: first, that IR is here to stay, but, second, that IR will keep evolving as the two disciplines that it relies on evolve—the practice of investment and the practice of corporate management. It is essential that IROs who desire long careers keep closely in touch with both of these constantly developing fields.

CHAPTER 3

The Ethics of Investor Relations

Investor relations (IR) is never ethically neutral. IR acts as a channel between two essential, productive and beneficial activities, and assists both of them: (1) the corporate task of creating customers, employment, and economic wealth and (2) the equity market task of helping the best companies grow and enabling a wide audience to benefit from corporate success.

The corporation is not simply a device for making profit for owners. Since the 16th century, corporations have played an essential part in the economic growth of European states. Corporations do not obtain moral purpose and a "social license" through acts of philanthropy. Corporations do not need to engage in charitable work because they have ready-made social purposes which are as great, if not greater, than any philanthropic endeavor they could participate in. Corporations contribute to society in four essential ways as shown in Figure 3.1.

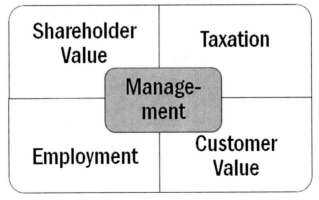

Figure 3.1 The four social functions of the public company

IR contributes directly to shareholder value but also facilitates a wider social purpose by keeping management informed. All four of these "social functions" of the corporation rely however on **profitability,** and since investors are a group keenly focused on profit, communication with investors is a key task of management.

IR facilitates disclosure, dialogue, understanding, and mutual adjustment. IR helps investors to play a positive role in corporations. Investors have a unique authority based on both the information and sanctions that they have access to. Investors may be the only group that can penetrate the ivory tower of management, and their broad commitment to overall firm success distinguishes them from the many sectional interests that management engages with. Investors represent the best source of business advice that management can access. Their knowledge of competitors, industry dynamics, and macroeconomic factors can be of great value. One does not have to agree with the "shareholder value" doctrine to believe that investors have a unique status and a unique role, and IR has a special responsibility to unlock the value from the shareholder relationship.

IR is part of the oil that helps the stock market function smoothly by matching investors with appropriate companies, keeping investor expectations realistic and ensuring that management teams are aware of investor sentiment. Capitalism has proven the only economic system that can provide the living standards and liberties that citizens of advanced nations expect, and so by helping to maintain efficient and fair equity markets, IR has a vital role in facilitating the growth of wealth and economic freedom, and the human rights and democratic institutions that have been shown to develop from sustained economic growth.

The Social Purpose of IR

By keeping management compliant, helping companies avoid valuation crises, informing management of market sentiment, and contributing to corporate strategy making, IR performs a valuable service to management which has wider benefits. By helping investors with the valuation process and keeping management in touch with investor sentiment, IR is serving investors but also serving the wider market. IR plays a part in maintaining market efficiency and price stability by ensuring that accurate corporate information flows to the market quickly, and that problems with corporate performance, activity, or strategy are fed to the management team while they still have time to make improvements, or correct perceptions. IR at its best can perform a valuable function of increasing market efficiency. The perception of market efficiency provides benefit to wider society by attracting investment to the national economy, by regularizing corporate performance and dividends, and by encouraging the public to invest and thus benefit from corporate wealth directly.

IR can contribute substantial value to corporations that take it seriously, but its value is not limited by the boundaries of the firm. IR serves a purpose beyond benefiting the participants in any single transaction, important though that purpose is. IR's benefits also flow to market participants generally and to the society beyond the stock market. IR has the potential to contribute on three levels as shown in Figure 3.2.

IR can make a contribution to the solution of three dilemmas:

1. The managerial dilemma—How can investors be satisfied?
2. The industrial dilemma—How can the asymmetry between investors and corporations be ameliorated?
3. The societal dilemma—How can national wealth be shared?

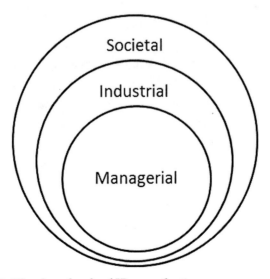

Figure 3.2 The three levels of IR contribution

The most obvious contribution that IR makes is to solve the managerial dilemma caused by the coincidence of the increase in investors' demands for information, interpretation, dialogue, and managerial action, and the increase in the regulation and scrutiny of that same communication with investors. IR was created as a professional function in order to satisfy these demands in a compliant, equitable, and efficient manner. The second and wider contribution that IR makes is to mitigate the corporate governance problems that affect advanced capitalism, and which are worsened as the investment chain lengthens, as corporate ownership fragments, and as business models and business networks grow increasingly complex. The third and widest contribution that IR can make is at a societal level. The industrial system is not designed as a self-serving ecosystem, but has wider responsibilities to share the wealth that it generates. It does this in several ways: through taxation, through employment, through efficiencies passed on to customers through price cuts, through improvements in product quality, through dividends, and through philanthropy. The contribution that IR makes to wider society is to make investment comprehensible, attractive, and, above all, safe for all investors. By communicating accurate information to all market participants and thus encouraging long-term investment from all investors small and large, IR helps to democratize the stock market and build public support for the system of economic freedom loosely called "capitalism."

Albert Hirschman conceived a very wide-ranging theory in 1970 in a book called: "Exit, Voice and Loyalty." Hirschman's basic idea is that members of social groups (whether customers, employees, shareholders, citizens, etc.) have two basic choices when their satisfaction with the group declines. They can either silently exit or else voice their concerns, in the hope of reforming the group. Which option is chosen depends on a number of factors, including exit costs, personality, feelings of loyalty, voice mechanisms etc. Hirschman developed his theory in a period when corporations were taking customer satisfaction and customer loyalty more seriously. He was one of the first economists to try to combine political and economic research methods. Economists before and since have focused on exit rather than on the process of voice, since exit is much easier to model. Organizations that want to avoid exit need to provide mechanisms for voice, whereas organizations that wish to avoid voice need to facilitate easy exit. All organizations should measure exit and voice carefully. Investors who are unhappy may use the press to voice their concerns, creating negative sentiment. Larger investors will find exiting their shareholdings difficult. An outflow of investors which is not replaced by new investors will produce a fall in the stock price. IROs therefore need to measure investor churn and investor sentiment, and take investor comments and grievances seriously before these opinions become public. IROs should facilitate private voice, survey investor sentiment regularly, and use careful marketing to ensure that new investors are comfortable with the firm's strategy and management.

Criticisms of IR

The four main criticisms of IR are as follows: (1) IR is not necessary because the stock market has an effective pricing mechanism; (2) IR is unfair because it promotes selective disclosure and penalizes the private shareholder; (3) it is wasteful and potentially corrupting for corporate officers to focus on the share price; their role is to manage the company, and the market will take care of the stock price; (4) IR is irresponsible. Stocks should not be "promoted" since they come with no guarantees and should be a serious and rational purchase.

The first criticism is commonly leveled at IR by finance and economics academics who subscribe to the efficient market hypothesis (EMH); the view that advanced stock markets (such as the London Stock Exchange and New York Stock Exchange) are informationally efficient and that investors cannot predict the markets, and nor can corporate managers improve their stock prices with "marketing" since the markets price in all relevant information immediately. Therefore, neither investors nor managers have anything to gain by making personal contact with each other.

The second criticism is that IR uses disreputable practices to manage share prices. The line between illegal practices such as insider trading and the "earnings game" is not always clear. These practices have been around since stock markets began, and it is unfair to condemn the IR profession as being the source of these practices; indeed, responsible IR practitioners may be the best hope of eliminating this sort of behavior. The belief that private meetings between managers and analysts are unfair on private investors was behind RegFD, which was generally supported by private shareholders and opposed by institutional investors. The meetings, however, are not all about managers disclosing to the investors and analysts, but also involve managers getting rebukes, advice, and other valuable feedback from representative owners and intelligent observers. So long as the golden rule is observed that no material nonpublic information should be disclosed in a private meeting, then these meetings perform a legitimate function as a channel of mutual enlightenment.

The third criticism is often leveled at corporate officers by investors. Investors often assert that the officers' role is to manage the business and not to value the stock, which is the role of the market. However, it is precisely the value of the chief executive officers and chief financial officers time that is one of the most powerful reasons for the existence of an IR function so that the role of the chief officers in promoting the company can be kept within strict limits. The prime factors in stock valuation are sustained corporate profitability, solid market position, and good prospects, and the markets' expectations of this profitability will not be lessened by any amount of proactive marketing of the stock. This criticism should be taken seriously and clear boundaries set for the IR time committed by the chief officers.

The final criticism is also very valid. IR does have a sales aspect, but selling a product is not the same as "pushing" it. IR requires a sensitive and fact-based selling process. "Promoting" the stock does not mean presenting just the virtues of the product, since company officers are not authorized to act as salespeople or advisors to investors. "Promotion" means firstly getting onto the radar of the investor, and secondly, facilitating the investor's appraisal of the company by making sure that corporate goals, corporate strategy, industry data, and evidence of executional skill are easily accessible to the investor.

CHAPTER 4

How the London Stock Exchange Works

The listed corporation deals with three main parties in the equity markets: sell-side analysts, investors, and financial journalists, as shown in Figure 4.1.

Analysts can be divided into three types:

Sell-side analysts have been an important feature of the U.S. equity markets since the 1920s, although they were not common in the United Kingdom's markets till the 1960s (Golding, 2003). They usually work for investment banks. Their job is to publish research on companies in order

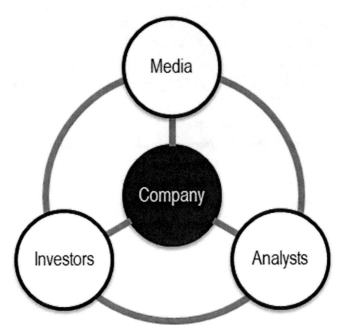

Figure 4.1 The company-equity market interface

to encourage the trading of its stock. They are remunerated according to the commissions they generate from their clients trading of stock. They are therefore attracted to large-cap stocks, with large daily trading volumes. Analysts each invest considerable time analyzing a small number of companies to provide earnings and valuation estimates. Analysts are the "financial detectives" of the financial markets (Kleinfield, 1985), with the average analyst covering 16 stocks (Groysberg, Healy, and Maber, 2011). Analysts are usually financially qualified and also pick up qualitative skills of assessing industry prospects, firm strategy, and management competence. Analysts, despite their problems (most notably their overfocus on large-cap stocks, a high degree of herd-instinct, and far from insignificant conflicts of interest), provide market efficiencies by circulating analysis on companies so that investors do not need to analyze every stock. The role of analysts is to produce forecasts of stock prices. In a stock market where all investors used the same measures of value, this might be achievable, but since so many different methodologies are in use, a stock price is nothing more than a market average of varying valuations, and so most stock prices are highly vulnerable to change. Predicting stock prices is therefore about as scientific as astrology, and valuing stock is something that investor relations (IR) departments should not assist with. Management should not even have a view on the company's stock price, but the prevalence of stock price triggered payments to managements (usually in the form of stock options) has blurred the line between the role of the markets (valuation) and the role of management (performance). It is the view of this author that the single most important cause of "earnings management" is the existence of stock price–related bonus schemes for executives. The truth of the stock markets is that valuations are nothing better than educated and collective (and often self-serving) guess work. Even the historical performance figures that are used, despite being the most objective part of corporate performance analysis, are somewhat subjective, as anybody trained in the compiling of financial statements knows:

> The accounts of a corporation carrying on a complex modern business are not, and cannot be, statements of absolute fact. They are necessarily based largely on conventions, on estimates, and on opinions . . . I have found from experience that it is by no means always fully appreciated even by people who might be supposed to be well versed in financial affairs. (May, 1932)

Small-cap stocks tend to be neglected by analysts, creating a vicious circle of poor publicity, which is somewhat alleviated by the role of fee-based research. Sell-side analysts represent the best-researched actors in the financial markets. They are the public face of IR because of the glamour of their work, their high profiles in the business press, and the semi-public nature of their research.

Senior analysts make between £150k and £400k, with a bonus of similar size based on commission and fund manager ratings. In November 2007, the Financial Services Authority unbundled commissions in their implementation of the EU's "Markets in Financial Instruments Directive I." Only execution costs and research could now be included in commission. The future of sell-side research is again in question since from Jan 2017 investment banks will be prohibited from paying for sell-side research out of commissions, one of the many changes included in "Markets in Financial Instruments Directive II."

Buy-side analysts are much more recent than sell-side analysts. The "widespread dissatisfaction with the quality of sell-side research" (Citigate Dewe Rogerson, 2014) by both companies and investors resulted in companies prioritising direct contact with investors, and investors conducting more of their own research, which is called "buy-side" research. Buy-side analysts were established in the 1990s by institutional investors because of the perceived bias in sell-side research. They tend to cover a larger number of stocks and produce less-detailed research, which is only for the use of the portfolio managers within the institutional investor in order to make investment decisions. Although the buy-side is less glamorous than the sell-side, since buy-side analysts do not have a public profile, their research is more objective and credible from the perspective of portfolio managers.

Fee-based research. Paid for research is utilized by small firms that do not have many sell-side analysts covering them. It varies in credibility and detail, but can be an important part of the marketing of small stocks.

Investors. The term *investor* is somewhat of a personification since investment decisions typically involve multiple people, but the key decision makers in investment management firms are usually entitled "portfolio managers" and manage a particular portfolio of investments within an investment management institution implementing its investment strategy and managing the day-to-day portfolio trading of securities on behalf of

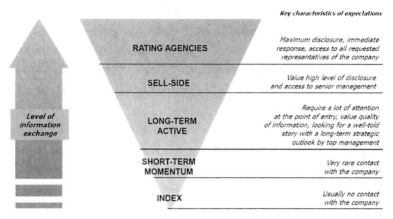

Figure 4.2 Stakeholder expectations (© BRE BANK SA 2009)

clients, in accordance with the investment objectives and parameters defined by those clients. Fees charged by investment managers to their clients are generally based on a percentage of client assets under management.

Media. Some investor relations officers (IROs) have responsibility for financial public relations, others don't. The financial press (the business pages of the quality press, investment magazines, and relevant trade press titles) can be very influential for reputation, especially for consumer businesses. Financial journalists tend to be very focused on headlines, much keener on bad news then good news, and not highly knowledgeable about business. Some CEOs would rather keep out of the press entirely, while some are very media friendly. IROs should follow their corporate traditions on this, and liaise closely with the director of communications.

A core principle of effective communication is to understand the needs of different audiences. Figure 4.2 shows the typical information requirements of different stakeholders; the bottom three are different types of investors, with analysts above them and rating agencies at the top.

Although all market participants have the right to equality of information, by knowing what different market participants are looking for, companies can assist their decision-making and obtain a more favorable response simply by ensuring that all investors have the information they need.

CHAPTER 5

Marketing and IR

The dominant paradigm within the field of corporate governance views all investors as "owners," while the managers are merely the agents of the investors. This "Corporate Governance Paradigm" (CGP) has developed in England since the great trading companies of the 1500s onward and is based on shareholders perceiving themselves as owners. The "relationship-marketing paradigm" (RMP) is very different. Investors are viewed as customers rather than owners, and managers have to capture, service, satisfy, and retain investors. In this paradigm, the managers behave like owners and pursue new investors.

Traditional economic theories about stock market efficiency suggest that the active marketing of corporate stock is unnecessary, since the market already incorporates all relevant factors into the stock price. Stock valuation is a highly complex art, however, with significant subjective elements, especially for stocks without significant financial history, and so marketing stocks to potential investors and information intermediaries is now generally regarded by corporations as being as essential as the marketing of their products to consumers. Many studies have shown the financial value of investor relations (IR) to corporations such as Lang and Lundholm (1996); Francis, Hanna, and Philbrick (1997); Holland (1998); Brennan and Tamaronski (2000); Bushee and Miller (2007); Agarwal, Bellotti, and Taffler (2009); Brennan and Kelly (2000); Gruner (2002); and Lev (1992).

There is wide divergence on what marketing is. According to Kotler and Keller (2011), marketing is "the art and science of choosing target markets and getting, keeping, and growing customers through creating, delivering, and communicating superior customer value."

The marketing concept has been extended by many writers from the 1950s onward[1] For example: Drucker (1954), Keith (1960), Kotler and Levy (1969), Lazer (1969), Kotler and Levy (1971), Kotler and Zaltman (1971), Kotler (1972), Kotler and Levy (1973), Kotler (1973), Kotler and Murray (1975), Kotler and Mindak (1978), Krapfel (1982), Houston (1986), McKenna (1991), and Webster (1994).

Unfortunately, the term *marketing* is often used in a pejorative sense in Europe, and so *proactive IR* is a more acceptable term among British investor relations officers (IROs). Marketing suggests selling, and selling is regarded as a low and dubious task in the United Kingdom. The term means something more positive in the United States, however, and National Investor Relations Institute (NIRI) has been unashamed to talk of the marketing content of IR from the start.

> Investor relations is a strategic management responsibility that integrates finance, communication, marketing and securities law compliance to enable the most effective two-way communication between a company, the financial community, and other constituencies, which ultimately contributes to a company's securities achieving fair valuation. (Adopted by the NIRI Board of Directors, March 2003.)

Nielsen and Bukh (2011) agree that "IR is fundamentally a marketing exercise in relation to the company's shares on the stock market." Marketers are skilled in demand management; this is more than just stimulating demand for their products. During the marketing concept debate of the 1970s, Kotler (1973) identified eight discrete tasks of marketing.

IROs require an understanding of the following four elements, each of which can be regarded as basic elements of the process of marketing and exchange:

1. How the **market** values stocks (the buying process)
2. How the **company** makes money (product characteristics)

---

[1]See Valentine (2013) for a summary of the many extensions of the marketing concept and suggestions for further extensions.

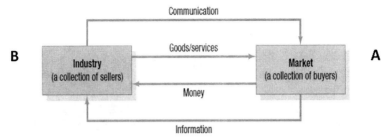

Figure 5.1 A model of marketing exchange (© Kotler and Keller 2011)

  3. What our **investors** want (customer satisfaction and retention)
  4. The **rules** of the marketplace (market regulation)

A model of marketing exchange (from Kotler and Keller, 2011) is shown in Figure 5.1:

In this exchange, A buys from B a product (that B owns) in exchange for payment (that B receives). The motivation of B is quite clear, while the motivation of A is more complex, but is usually defined as receiving "value."

The marketing of corporate stock deviates from this usual pattern, since for secondary market sales (the vast majority of stock transfers) the company does not own the stock and will not receive payment for it. Companies, however, do actively promote the second-hand market in their own stock, for a number of reasons. The product has a perpetual and non-deteriorating nature. The purchase of stock starts a legal relationship, not with the seller but with the company. The value of the company is decided in the secondary markets, not the primary markets.

Except in the case of initial public offerings and rights issues when new stocks are offered to the public, firms are not involved in the exchange of stocks to the buyer nor receive any money from the sale of stocks; this is done by the stock exchange itself on behalf of the buyer and seller. The firm acts only in a communication capacity. The secondary market is thus a peer-to-peer second-hand market, like eBay. IR has just two of the common four elements of the marketing mix—product and promotion—as the stock exchange takes care of both the price and the

Consumer Marketing	Investor Marketing
Price set by seller	Little influence on price
Primary market	Second-hand market
B2C	B2B
Light regulation	Heavy regulation
Exchange	No exchange
Performance claims essential and guarantees common	No guarantees and performance claims highly restricted
Product has a finite life	Product is perpetual
Transaction (product) based	Relationship (ongoing service) based
Advertising is important	Advertising prohibited

Figure 5.2 Consumer and investor marketing compared

distribution. Figure 5.2 lists some of the key differences between IR and consumer marketing:

IR is an intangible, non-exchange, single-product, secondary market form of marketing.

Effective IR has a large element of marketing in it, although there are also non-marketing roles. The following core marketing concepts are essential in IR: (1) understanding the decision-making unit (DMU) and the decision-making process (DMP); (2) Segmentation, targeting, and positioning (STP; a marketer can rarely satisfy everyone in a market; therefore, marketers segment the market); (3) relationship marketing; (4) aiming for customer satisfaction and repeat business (or retention); (5) matching product characteristics with customers buying criteria; (6) using market research to gather intelligence on all the points above, rather than relying on habit or presumption; (7) that personal selling is an essential part of the investment process for many institutional investors.

Common marketing terms such as *marketing, sales,* and *customer* are not customarily used, but this merely shows the ubiquity and specificity of marketing and the fact that marketing techniques are regarded as an essential part of every professional practice, although the word "marketing" is rarely used.

The core of the marketing concept, however, is not an array of particular techniques, but acceptance of the marketing philosophy, which is *the recognition within the enterprise of its dependence on the goodwill and satisfaction of its customers for its own survival.* Investors from the 1930s to the 1950s were largely taken for granted due to managerial hegemony, poor liquidity, and restrictions on investors. It was the shake-up of the United Kingdom stock exchange by the takeovers of the 1980s that produced a sudden interest by corporate executives in investor opinion and the recruiting of IROs who could interpret the signs of the financial markets and warn of crises before they hit.

Increasing diversity of investors. In classical abstract economic analysis, all shareholders have the same requirements. In fact this is far from the case. Investors are quite diverse, and the trend is toward greater diversity. Several aspects of diversity are worth mentioning:

A) **Geographical diversity.** That is, the foreign ownership of domestic stock markets. Forty percent of the London Stock Market is now owned by non-UK-registered institutions. This can place an extra burden on the firm as foreign investors may require a general education in the firm's business model, products, and markets. On the other hand, foreign investors may be very low maintenance since the distance makes meetings with management less feasible.

B) **Ethical diversity.** The growth of "ethical investing" of different types is a notable feature of the modern stock exchange. The screening methods of such funds differ widely, as do the ethical rules of ordinary funds.

C) **Philosophical diversity.** This includes a number of other aspects such as focus on income or capital growth, form of pre-purchase analysis (fundamental or technical), usual length of investment horizon, stock picking or index tracking, and the degree of "activism."

It is this degree of diversity that allows the IRO to engage in the most characteristic aspect of modern marketing, the art of segmentation.

CHAPTER 6

Principles of Corporate Reputation and Investor Communication

Corporate Reputation

Investor relations (IR) is an important component of the reputational management of a listed corporation. As Figure 6.1 shows, reputational management has three essential elements: firm behavior (including financial performance), firm communications, and the communication that other parties have about the firm. This model neatly represents the three

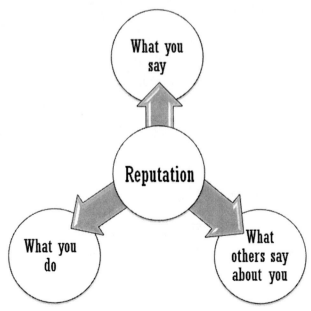

Figure 6.1 The reputational model

ways that the financial community learns about firms: by engaging with firm behavior directly through financial reports, by listening to what the firm says about its own performance, and by engaging with intermediaries who have opinions on firm performance.

The three elements have different levels of credibility; firm behavior possesses the highest level of credibility, followed by the interpretations of external experts, with firm communications having the lowest level of credibility. No amount of positive communication by the firm can overcome poor results or bad behavior; firm communications in this scenario will be seen as "spin." The performance of the firm is generally seen as being outside of the realm of IR, which is principally a communication function, but IR plays an essential role in corporate valuation both by managing the views of analysts and by ensuring that firm communications are as accurate and helpful as possible to the investment community.

Communications Skills

Communication skills are often imperceptible and thus hard to define, but the core communication skills that investor relations officers (IROs) need to learn include the following:

- Careful timing of communication
- Selection of the right channel(s) for the characteristics of the message (such as complexity and speed) and the targeted audience
- Clarity and maximum simplicity
- Use of the right "tone" and emphasis
- Consistency of information across multiple channels
- Intelligent selection, illustration, evidencing and sequencing of information to craft a coherent, credible and engaging story

Distinctive Features of the Marketing of Corporate Stock

This book suggests that marketing is a useful paradigm for analyzing much of the job of the IRO, although the traditional way of thinking about marketing needs to be extended in order to accommodate the distinctive features of financial products.

The marketing of corporate stock is different from the marketing of consumer products and similar to the marketing of financial services in the following seven ways:

1. Intangible—Banking and financial products are abstract and cannot be touched.
2. Complex—Products such as derivatives, documentary credits, or loan facilities require detailed explanation to corporate or institutional clients.
3. Lengthy decision-process—Banking and financial products are not bought lightly, or on impulse, and so they need to be sold in a special way.
4. Trust—The City takes its definition of trust very seriously. Financial relationships are often built over a long period of time and are very sensitive to changes in mutual trust.
5. Intermediation—Intermediaries are commonplace because of the complexity of the product.
6. Regulation—The promotion and sale of the product is highly regulated, as is any communication regarding the product.
7. Inequality—Not all buyers are equal or desirable. A bank for instance may decline a customer because their income or character is insufficiently good.

In addition to the seven features above, the marketing of corporate stock is different from the marketing of other financial services in the following 10 major ways:

1. The marketing of corporate stock does not involve direct exchange between the corporation and the investor.
2. Each company sells only one product (presuming a single class of stock).
3. The stock of products on the market is fixed. Companies have to obtain approval from shareholders for the issue of additional stock.
4. The company does not set the price of the stock; this is set by an auctioning process managed by the stock exchange.
5. The promotion and sale of stocks are both highly regulated, as is any communication regarding the stocks. Heavy penalties apply

for breaches of these rules. The most important rules include the following:

a. Promises regarding stock performance or any suggestions of value are prohibited.

b. There is no ability to prevent particular people from buying your company's stocks, the markets are perfectly open, and purchase and sale may take place at any time when the market is open.

c. All potential buyers and current holders are entitled to equality of treatment by the company, whether they hold millions of stocks or just a single stock. Complete openness of communication. The whole market sees your communication with investors as all information must be publicly available.

6. Customers are not equal in significance. A single customer could purchase all of the available stock if the holders are willing to sell. In most cases, listed firms have only a relatively small number of significant shareholders. For instance, BP plc, the third biggest listed company on the London Stock Exchange (January 2014), has 1,610 significant shareholders (figures as on December 12, 2012, www.bp.com) defined as shareholders with over 100,000 shares each. These shareholders, who represent 0.5 percent of the number of shareholders, collectively own 96.7 percent of the company. The remaining 3.3 percent of the company is composed of 295,000 shareholders, representing 99.5 percent of shareholders. Even the largest listed companies with highly dispersed ownerships therefore need only the support of a tiny proportion of the investors in the market; the firm does not have to please the market at large, but only a small proportion of it.

7. In addition to the official rules, very rigid cultures prevail in the old stock exchanges such as London. The market, for instance, puts a great deal of value on consistency, regularity and predictability in communication, and in companies meeting targets precisely. The markets are in a word highly conservative, and exhibit strong norms and herd behavior.

8. Highly geographically concentrated buyers. Investors and analysts are concentrated in the financial centers of London, New York, Frankfurt, Boston, etc.

9. Buyer homogeneity. Investors and analysts are overwhelmingly male, aged 25 to 50, intelligent, academically well qualified, urban, in the top 10 percent of the population for wealth, politically conservative, English speaking, and highly numerate. (Junkus and Berry, 2010)

10. Diversity of customer needs and product usage. Some investors will hold the stock for a few seconds; others for decades. Some investors will push for dividends; others are interested purely in capital growth. Investors will have different ideas on capital structure and strategy. Some investors will make regular contact; others will never communicate. Some investors will try to influence strategy; others will simply observe.

The Characteristics of Communication Channels

Channels of communication differ in their characteristics. A key skill that finance specialists need to learn if they are responsible for IR is the differences between these various channels, since these differences have important practical, ethical, and legal implications. A few key characteristics of communication channels are as follows:

1. Speed. The time it takes from the point at which the sender feeds the information into the system until all the users receive it.

2. Sophistication. The extent to which complex data can be presented. Complex data include tables, charts, and diagrams.

3. Integrity. The extent to which information is preserved in the form that the sender specifies.

4. Credibility. The extent to which the channel is perceived as reliable by the users.

5. Reach. The number of users who access the message.

6. Access. Whether messages can be picked up for free by any interested parties or whether the messages are restricted, for instance, on payment of a fee, or restricted to users who have a certain status.

7. Permanence. Whether the channel stores past messages and allows users to access these past messages.

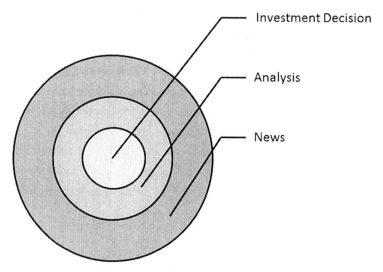

Figure 6.2 The IR onion

Investment does not take place purely based on an investor's examination of corporate data; it takes place within a context of corporate reputation and news. Figure 6.2 shows the "IR onion" which demonstrates the two layers of analysis that investors need to penetrate before they invest: the layer of news and the layer of analysis from sell-side analysts. The outer layer of general news coverage is publically available and generally shallow in nature. The inner layer is provided by analysts, and is far more expert and detailed. Both of these layers provide both a positive and a negative function for listed companies. The positive function is the publicity that they provide to stocks which they report, which facilitates the market's awareness of the stock. The negative function is the ability of both types of coverage to reveal the weaknesses, problems, and risks faced by the company. Both layers are independent of management and, therefore, both high in credibility and low in controllability, creating a real hazard for management if negative sentiment emerges.

CHAPTER 7

Crafting an Investment Thesis

Crafting the Corporate Strategy

The investor relations officer (IRO) has an important role in helping craft the corporate strategy and the corporate story, and then conveying strategy and story to investors and financial media.

Corporate strategy now represents the difference between success and failure. Prior to the competitive pressures of the 1970s, many organizations did not possess "strategies," simply collections of different businesses and products. Many British businesses were hopelessly diversified; others were overfocused on single market niches.

The traumas of the 1970s saw the return to a more conservative style of management as the confident belief that markets would be ever-expanding evaporated. Conglomerates were encouraged by consultants and investors to slim down and focus on a narrower range of activities. A new generation of business leaders emerged who were focused on shareholder returns, corporate strategy, and organizational transformation. The weakening of trade union power allowed models of rapid organizational change to reemerge, although this was too late to save some British businesses. At the same time, a report by Lee and Tweedie (1977) suggested that accounting information was incomprehensible to many investors and should be supplemented by narrative content.

In the United Kingdom, financial analysts quickly adopted the new methods of strategic analysis such as Porter's Five Forces (Porter, 1980). The growth of the consultancy industry and the rise of the MBA circulated the new views on corporate strategy. Peters and Waterman in 1982 published a new type of strategy book that blended academic research with corporate case studies and offered bite-size nuggets of corporate advice along with universal principles of good strategy. The book developed a cult following and sold three million copies within four years.

Henry Mintzberg (1987) wrote about the difference between strategy as plan and strategy as pattern. Strategy is not just what the organization intends to do (the strategic plan) but also the pattern of existing activity. If observers see a difference between strategy as preached and strategy as practiced, then the organization's strategic credibility will suffer. Another danger is that short-term strategies to take advantage of current opportunities (what Mintzberg calls "ploys") may compromise the long-run strategic direction of the organization. The listed company is in the fortunate position of being carefully monitored by analysts, investors, and journalists who are looking for inconsistencies in what the organization says and what it does, or between what the organization does in one place and what it does in another place. The firm has to monitor itself as carefully as outside observers monitor it, and the IRO is in a key position to guard the consistency of the corporate strategy and the corporate story.

As Figure 7.1 demonstrates, strategic choice is based on two prior assessments: the assessment of internal capabilities and the assessment of the environment of the firm, both the industry environment and the wider macroeconomic environment that all firms face. Results however, which is what investors are ultimately seeking, also depend on successful implementation. Therefore, disappointing results raise the question of whether the strategy was at fault or whether the problem is one of implementation. In order for results forecasts to be credible, corporations must convince analysts and investors that they have competence in implementation in addition to their strategic choice being based on solid analysis.

Corporations will find that certain analysts and investors can give great insight into their industry environments because of their access to macroeconomic analysis from professional economists (which firms rarely have direct access to) and because of their access to the management teams of competing firms. One of the greatest benefits of good relations with analysts and investors is the opening up of two-way communication which can yield helpful industry and macro-level intelligence for the management team.

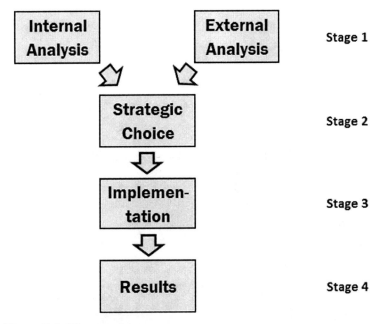

Figure 7.1 The strategy process

This author has read dozens of strategy textbooks, but has never found one that referred to the strategic preferences of investors, or one that outlined a workable process of consulting with investors. Many companies seem to leave consultation with investors till a very late stage of strategy formulation, either for fear of "selective disclosure" or because investors are not regarded as having a useful contribution to the process. We suggest that it is highly advisable to both consider the general perspective of investors and to consult with key investors before publication. The general strategic preferences of fund managers are discussed by Golding (2003: 166) and include the following:

- Good numbers
- Growth potential—in a growing market
- Simple ownership structure
- "Pure play"—a simple business
- Simple corporate story—e.g., "growth" or "recovery"
- Simple and convincing strategy

- Merger and acquisition potential
- Size—larger firms preferred, ideally dominating the profitable segments of their market
- Quality products—differentiation strategy rather than competing on price
- Management team with a record of delivery

Crafting the Corporate Story

Storytelling is a natural and powerful method of communication. The human mind connects events chronologically and causally, and stories provide these connections in ready-made form. A story can be defined as a narrative of events in a generally chronological form, with certain events, people, and moments emphasized to provide meaning. Stories provide reassurance to people since stories are easily comprehensible and memorable and most people believe themselves to be very capable of testing narrative fidelity, that is, whether the story "rings true" or not (Rentz, 1992). Narrative is central to western culture. For instance, children are taught using stories from an early age, and the untangling of events into a clear chronology is also an essential part of the trial of a case in the law courts, and so the practice of using narrative both to understand and to communicate is very familiar.

Storytelling is an essential part of many professions, with journalists, lawyers, police officers, historians, and biographers all needing the skill of finding and piecing together facts to create a meaningful narrative. Differences in access to information, selection, juxtaposition, and emphasis will change the meaning of the story. Despite their quantitative bias, investors and analysts share this cultural love of stories. Additionally, analysts, while needing to demonstrate objectivity and mastery of detail, also need "an angle" for their commentary. The analyst is part number cruncher, but also part journalist. Each piece they write has to have a purpose and a point, and this is why the "story" element is so important for analysts. While skilled users of the financial statements and company announcements can craft a substantial part of the corporate story given enough time, many analysts and investors do not have the time or resource to work from the ground up at forming their own narrative. While some analysts and investors are highly autonomous and will build their

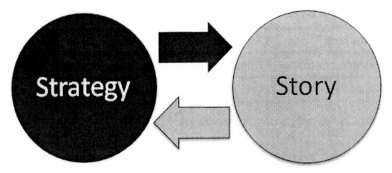

Figure 7.2 The interdependence of strategy and story

own understanding of the company from scratch, many others want help and shortcuts to understanding. If the company presents a credible and evidenced story to analysts and investors, then that story can become the received wisdom of the financial community.

Simple stories are best. Golding (2003:169) suggests that there are a very limited number of effective investment stories, the main ones being "growth", "new management/recovery," and "industry consolidation".

As Figure 7.2 shows, the corporate story is not merely a passive narrative based on corporate strategy. The process of shaping a credible corporate story will involve making improvements to the corporate strategy. The result of this process is a combined corporate strategy story that generates both internal and external support and sustainable corporate profit.

The first test of the combined corporate strategy story is whether it can hold up under internal criticism, the second test is whether it can hold up under the criticism of trusted stakeholders, the third test is whether it can hold up under public scrutiny, and the fourth and ultimate test is whether it can hold up over time and the pressure of a changing environment.

The corporate story is not simply a tale of what might happen. The management team need a corporate story that can connect past, present, and future. While CEOs love to talk about their plans for the future, analysts will want to ground forward projections on an understanding of the current business and the management's team's past record at delivering results.

Since the early 1980s investor and analysts have expected managements to talk the languages of strategy and implementation as well as the language of financial results. These three subjects can be blended together as shown in Figure 7.3 to craft the corporate story. The story includes

Past	Present	Future
1 Strategy	4 Strategy	7 Strategy
2 Implementation	5 Implementation	8 Implementation
3 Results	6 Results	9 Results

Figure 7.3 Crafting the investment story

past, present, and future actions since corporate strategy emerges from an understanding of the corporation's past and present. The corporate story is a sense-making narrative which turns isolated facts into a coherent and attractive pattern of activity.

Figure 7.3 shows how the strategic process can be converted into a story. Past strategy, present strategy, and future strategy are weaved into a story, using stages 2, 3, and 4 of Figure 7.1 for each time period. Of the three elements of the story, "implementation" is the one most difficult to ascertain from corporate documents, and this is where analysts can add most value, through their face-to-face meetings with management. Assessments of implementation ability are subjective, but tend to involve judgments of management team track records, the ability of management to answer questions on current projects, the availability of good management information to support corporate decision-making, and the quality of the layer of managers immediately below the executive board. This team of managers are responsible for implementing management plans and will also represent the succession plan, being the executive board of the future. In this subjective assessment, analysts will tend to have personal methods of research and "rules of thumb," and it is worth speaking to analysts to discover what their assessments of management quality are based on.

The other characteristic of the story is that it should be current. A corporate story is not like a classic novel that satisfies readers for generations; it needs to be updated when the environment changes, or when goals are reached.

Analysts and journalists supply investors with ideas, facts, and opinions, which forms the raw material of much of investor decision-making. A company that refuses to communicate with analysts and journalists is giving them the power to shape the company's profile. To quote Hobor (1997) "not communicating takes the message out of the control of the company and puts it in the hands of others."

CHAPTER 8

Crafting the Investor Marketing Strategy

Investor relations (IR) is not an administrative activity, but a highly flexible discipline that needs to be guided with a clear strategy. The IR strategy model shown in Figure 8.1 presents the four strategic choices that the IR function faces. IR strategy is the combination of these four decisions:

1. Disclosure level
2. Degree of targeting

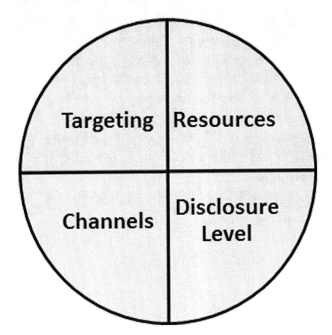

Figure 8.1 The IR strategy model

3. Selection of disclosure channels and
4. Level of resource

Disclosure Level

Disclosure level refers to the amount of information that is disclosed above and beyond the legally required information. Investors are asking IR officers for ever more information. Ninety-one percent of corporations worldwide provide extra information to investors. Effective disclosure remains the raison d'être of the IR function.

Degree of Targeting

Targeting is the essence of modern marketing. No product can satisfy the entire market, because customers have different desires, preferences, incomes, intellects, and lifestyles. Nor can the corporation afford to individually customize products for any but the most significant customers. The answer for most products lies in between these two extremes of perfect homogeneity and perfect heterogeneity, with segmentation and targeting. Segmentation is the process of dividing the market into groups, each group being united by similarity according to at least one significant variable. The firm then chooses one or more of these segments and develops a specialized marketing mix for each segment. In IR, targeting means deciding which investors fit best with the stock; which investors are most likely to buy the stock and then exhibit positive behaviour, such as holding the stock for a long period, and being generally supportive of corporate strategy.

In markets for long term financial products, the "quality" of customers is often important, since a purchase begins a long -term relationship between seller and buyer. The seller is looking for the right kind of buyer, not just any interested buyer.

Channel Selection

There are four principal channels for corporate information as shown in Figure 8.2: analysts, the media, direct contact with investors, and public disclosure. The mix of channels used will depend on the complexity of

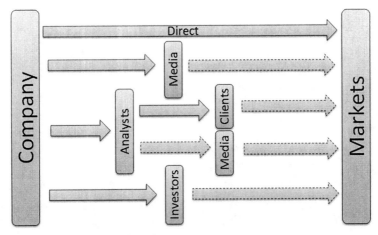

Figure 8.2 Channels of disclosure

the information, the credibility of each channel, the ability of the channel to transmit the information in a clear and secure way; and the reach (i.e., audience) of each channel. Increasingly, companies are communicating directly with investors and disintermediating analysts and journalists. The dotted arrows represent communication that is not controlled by the firm. The firm only retains complete control with direct communication, all other forms of communication involve uncertainty about whether messages will be delivered in the desired form.

Level of Resource

IR resource commitment is a sign of the influence that investors have in the corporation. Resources consist chiefly of not the IR personnel, but the time given to the IR function by the chief executive officer (CEO) and chief financial officer. The Chairman and Senior Independent Director (SID) may also have significant roles, but customarily these officers only get involved if the investors are unhappy with the performance of the CEO.

CHAPTER 9

Executing the Strategy

The Two-Stage Model of Investor Marketing

The two-stage model of marketing shown in Figure 9.1 utilizes two complimentary methods of stage one marketing: (1) targeting of investors and (2) corporate promotion. These two methods are designed to generate plenty of enquiries and opportunities for stage two marketing. Stage two then works with the investors to guide them through the valuation process which enables them to invest.

Both targeting and promotion rely on the firm having an agreed, consistent, and compelling story and brand identity and careful micro-segmentation (see Chapter 4 of Coe, 2004 for more information on micro-segmentation). Segmentation is essential for the effective use of targeting and also for networking and conference work, as the large number of investment-related conferences means that careful selection is essential.

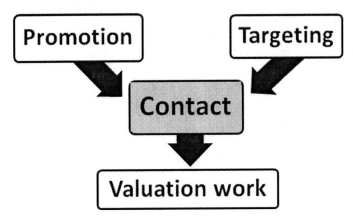

Figure 9.1 The two-stage model of investor marketing

Identifying Targets

Where does a company get its ideas about which investors it should target? The corporate network of brokers and analysts will provide ideas, although there are problems with their recommendations, since both often get paid for arranging these meetings.

What does a good investor look like? A formula for a good investor may look something like this:

$$IS = EL \times EI \times ESR$$

In this example, the overall investor score (IS) is a multiple of three factors: the expected longevity of the investment (EL), the expected size of the investment (EI), and the expected service ratio (ESR) which is the ratio between the cost of servicing an investor (such as time spent meeting the investor) and the benefits received from that investor (such as useful strategic feedback). Once the investor relations officer (IRO) has formed a clear idea of what constitutes good investor behavior, then he can begin a search for those characteristics.

Search methods include (a) good media monitoring. Following up any comments about your firm or industry, if they are critical, then you may be able to correct any misunderstandings, and if they are positive, then this might be a good time to schedule a presentation to that investor or analyst to convert a positive comment into a sale, and (b) regularly analyzing your share register to benchmark the profile of your shareholder register against that of your peers. From this analysis consider which segments of the investor community you should target. Then identify the investors who are most likely to want a long-term relationship, and then identify the decision makers within each of the investors. The direct approach then requires making personal contact by phone or e-mail with a target investor and offering to meet to present the corporate case personally.

Promotion—the Four Ways of Getting Noticed

As well as seeking out specific investors, the firm should raise its general profile so that investors notice it and approach it. Good marketing requires a deep understanding of product characteristics, consumer needs,

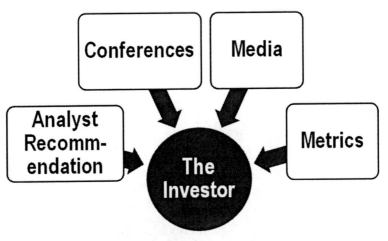

Figure 9.2 Four methods of getting investor attention

and how the product characteristics satisfy the consumer's needs. In a stock universe of tens of thousands of stocks, getting noticed and onto the radar of investors is the first essential step in getting a full valuation. The four ways of getting noticed by investors are shown in Figure 9.2.

The four methods for appearing on investors' radar are (1) using conferences and other events to present the company's case and meet investors directly, (2) obtaining a favorable media profile and getting noticed through positive news stories in those media channels respected by investors, (3) getting recommendations from financial analysts, and (4) getting through investors quantitative screens by performing well in one or more of the financial metrics that investors use to reduce the stock universe into a "long list" of stocks that are worth further analysis (for instance yield or P/E).

These four methods are all stage **one** marketing. Stage **two** marketing involves personally walking an analyst or investor through the valuation process. During the process of assisting an analyst or investor with their valuation model, it may be necessary to provide information that is not already in the public domain. This is a sensitive process that should be managed by the IRO to avoid the selective disclosure of material information. Raising disclosure levels is an important part of a stock promotion strategy, but needs to be handled with care as the markets generally expect extra disclosure to be maintained in perpetuity.

The Sales Role

As well as a **marketing** role, the IRO has a specific **sales** role. Sales has been defined as: "an interpersonal confrontation where at least one party has the aim of influencing an exchange" (Buttle, 1986).

There are several personal encounters between company management and investors:

- The results briefing
- The one-on-one investor meeting
- The one-on-one analyst meeting
- The small group meeting (usually analysts but could be smaller investors also)

Each of these meetings has a different personality depending on a number of factors including the following:

- The number of people involved
- What stage in the buying process the participants are at
- How positive the participants are about the stock
- The corporate performance context
- The macroeconomic context

The face-to-face meeting is still an important event in the investment process, despite the role of technology. Although many index investors will not request meetings, for other investors the meeting is an important stage in the investment decision. In addition to the information that may be communicated in the meeting, the meeting has a symbolic function; it is an indication to the investors that management regards them as important, and analysts value the meetings for the credibility that personal meetings give them with their own clients. For management, meetings represent opportunities to:

- Demonstrate their knowledge of the firm and its market
- Establish rapport with investors
- Understand the financial community better

- Impress investors with intellectual ability and personality
- Correct misperceptions

Although meetings are effectively interviews or trials, with one side requesting information and the other side providing it, at their best they are exercises in mutual understanding where management also gains information:

- What does the market think about our company?
- What does the market think of our current strategy?
- Who is the most positive and most skeptical of our analysts?
- What are the big obstacles to investment?
- How do they compare us with our competitors?
- What risks does the market associate with our company?
- How is the economy likely to develop in the future?
- What social trends and other macro factors will shape the market in the next few years?
- What investment philosophies guide our main investors?

Managements may find that certain investors, who combine industry knowledge with openness, may provide a useful sounding board on proposed projects, policy changes, and other corporate initiatives. Testing ideas in private with a few investors is a way of de-risking corporate decision-making, although the company must take care to avoid disclosing material information.

Meetings should always be documented. Formal results meetings must now be audio recorded (or video recorded depending on management/investor preference) and posted online so that all investors have the chance to listen to management, and so new investors can see the past few meetings. For the smaller events, we suggest that the IRO documents the questions asked and the answers given. At least two corporate officers should always be present when meeting with investors, analysts, or journalists. In some circumstances, the IRO may meet with small investors alone, although this is less than ideal, but even then some notes must be taken. The notes of questions asked serve as a very valuable log of investor/analyst interest and attitude. Clearly, it is very useful when preparing for meetings with an investor or analyst to have a record of the questions they asked last time the company met with them. The notes also have value for psychological purposes (the mere fact that notes are taken will help prevent company officers disclosing material information) and for compliance purposes (to act as a defense if the company is accused of selective disclosure).

Meetings tend to follow a three-step pattern with a descending degree of formality:

1. The pitch
2. The Q&A
3. The mingle

Viewed as a sales call, the investor/analyst meeting is somewhat different from normal business-to-business selling:

- The investor will not make a decision to buy during the encounter.
- The investor's decision may never be known.
- The company management is not authorized to give investment advice; they cannot recommend that the investor buy their stock.
- The company is not actually selling anything; the investor will buy from an existing owner of stock. That is, the company is effectively promoting the second-hand market in its own stock.
- The audience uses the meeting to gauge the quality of management, which is the one thing that the financial results don't tell them. Some of the questions may be asked not so much for the conveyance of information, but as tests of managerial knowledge, intellectual ability, and overall competence.
- The meeting is heavily driven by explanation of historic accounting numbers and policies, and also by expectations of future corporate performance.

But in other respects, the investor relations investor meeting is like a typical sales call:

- The seller will make a pitch, covering recent events, corporate strengths, and any objections that the investor is thought to have.
- After the pitch, there will be a series of questions from the investor.
- Management will highlight the strengths of the product, but also handle objections.
- The aim of the meeting is for the audience to be more positive about the product at the end of the meeting than they were at the start.

One-to-one meetings are likely to remain an essential part of the investment process because of both side's preferences for privacy. Solomon and Soltes (2013) found that private meetings are still productive for U.S. investors, despite RegFD, and especially for hedge funds who have greater flexibility in their trading patterns, and are able to make full use of the intelligence that they gather in these meetings.

CHAPTER 10

Introducing the Internet

The first web browser was launched in 1991 by Tim Berners-Lee, but it was with the launch of Mosaic in 1993 (which allowed the display of text and graphics on the same page), and the start of online shopping, with the launch of eBay and Amazon in 1994 and 1995, respectively, that web usage began to grow rapidly. Pages gradually became more interactive and allowed user-generated content and syndication (often called Web 2.0).

The Internet has had a substantial impact on both the practice of investing and the practice of investor relations (IR), due to its ability to give worldwide access to information within seconds. The Internet allows rapid communication at low cost, and so is inherently attractive as a communication tool. It also allows equality of access, a "level playing field" (what Bonson and Flores (2011) call "an unprecedented process of technological democratization"), and so can avoid the problem of "selective disclosure" which is inherent in meetings (even public meetings) and phone calls. Aspects of the Internet were rapidly adopted by companies for their IR programs (see Brennan and Kelly, 2000) Other benefits include the reduced executive time spent answering investor and analyst questions, the reduced costs of meetings and printed materials, and improved ability to communicate widely at short notice. The "broadcasting" function of the Internet was quickly utilized by corporations during the 1990s.[1] The "two-way" communication potential of the Internet has seen much more limited use (Deller, Stubenrath, and Weber, 1999, Bollen, Hassink, and Bozic, 2006). While Fama's "efficient market" (1965) is still far from being achieved (and seems unlikely ever to be achieved due to informational asymmetries and psychological factors), the Internet has

---

[1]Early U.K. studies include Lymer and Tallberg (1997), Hussey et al. (1998), Craven and Marston (1999), Deller, Stubenrath, and Weber (1999).

certainly brought the markets closer to this ideal, both in speed and in availability of relevant information. The limitations of traditional financial information also became more apparent as investment horizons contracted and methods of valuing nonfinancial assets became more widespread. Other corporate functions such as HR and marketing began to measure their value and contributed to the view that periodic, historical, cost-based, financial statements are no longer sufficient for making capital market decisions (Elliot 1992).

While the usefulness and growing importance of interactive digital platforms have been widely acknowledged, the IR function seems unsure about how to grasp the potential. Releasing information via Twitter, Facebook, and similar channels must be done with caution to avoid violating financial markets regulations. Moreover, companies are vulnerable to negative publicity that can be quickly and widely disseminated over social media networks, even if the company in question is not an active participant in social media.

Gowthorpe (2004) provides a snap shot of use of the Internet to disclose financial information to investors. At the time Gowthorpe's research was conducted (2001), although the Internet was well established, only about half of the companies analyzed had progressed to stage one, and there was very little evidence of video content. Gowthorpe (2004) also found that most companies did not consult with users on the information that they desired.

Additionally, investors and analysts may use their impressions of the quality of online disclosure and the responsiveness of the organization to requests for further information, to draw conclusions about the quality of corporate IT, financial reporting systems, and management in general; a practice defended by Bollen (2008).

The challenge for listed organizations is how to build effective (and compliant) relationships with key investors in an environment where "loyalty" is apparently ever decreasing (Falkow, 2010). In the face of reducing loyalty, companies must resist the temptation to reciprocate by reducing investment in the corporate side of the interface, and must strengthen their proposition in order to stand out from generic offerings. Leading corporations show that this can be done, and that improving the online offering is a core requirement if this goal is to be achieved.

CHAPTER 11

Using Traditional Online Channels

We will examine the main applications of traditional online media in investor relations (IR) below.

Online Annual Report

Despite many predictions of its decline, the annual report remains the single most important source of corporate information (ACCA, 2013) as Figure 11.1 illustrates, with 63 percent of investors surveyed regarding it as the most valuable input to the investment decision.

The annual report has been the dominant document of corporate performance for listed companies since the Companies Act of 1900.[1] As the number of stocks in investment portfolios has grown, having a single source of information has become even more vital. Annual reports have also changed, with more qualitative content.

Investors and analysts differ in their preferred method of reading corporate information, but traditional forms dominate according to ACCA (2013), with the online static report as the favored format (54 percent) with printed reports not far behind (45 percent). According to ACCA (2013), 45 percent of surveyed investors are using XBRL (eXtensible Business Reporting Language). The main benefits of XRBL is the ability to extract performance data in a standard format and thus compare performance between companies more easily, although there remains a lack of standardization in the use of taxonomies.

---

[1]The Joint Stock Companies Act of 1844 introduced a mandatory balance sheet, but this requirement was removed in 1856, until the 1900 Company Act. (Maltby, 1998)

Figure 11.1: Which of the following sources of information are most valuable for you as an input for decisions about investing in a company?

Figure 11.1 Information required by investors (© ACCA 2013)

IR Microsite

IR microsites are now well established as the primary places for current and historic investor information. The corporate IR microsite should be well publicized as the place where all material investor information will be uploaded.

Investor Information Packs (IIPs)

IIPs are a useful tool, being a compendium of the most helpful resources for an investor starting the fundamental analysis stage. They usually consist of relevant presentations and performance reports, and include specialized documents such as corporate history and product overviews. Compressing the most useful documents into a zip file for easier downloading is the usual practice.

IR Newsletter

A monthly e-mail newsletter containing links to relevant news stories, reports, and video content is a helpful way of keeping analysts and investors informed. Each e-mail should contain an "unsubscribe" link to allow recipients to quickly discontinue the service when they no longer need it.

Video Content

In addition to the annual report, the use of videos on the IR microsite is now common. With the growth of international investing, this is a helpful way of allowing remote investors to make some assessment of the quality and style of the corporate officers. The most common content is a 5 to 10 minute interview with the CEO following the results presentation. This is helpful to local analysts and investors who missed the results, international investors, and also private investors who would not have been able to access the results presentation.

Live Web Conferencing

Web conferencing is now an established method for connecting remote investors to your results presentations and other corporate events, as well as enabling investors to explore the history of corporate presentations through an accessible archive. Whether remote participants should be able to ask questions in the Q&A slot is something that companies have different policies on, but is worth investigating. Whether the Q&A slot should be recorded and uploaded is another policy choice which should be decided following consultation with participants, who may value privacy.

Search Engine Advertising

A few companies (such as BP plc, see Figure 11.2) do utilize search engine advertising to ensure that they are prominent in the search results for any related terms and to take people direct to the relevant page. This practice is worth experimenting with to see if it has a noticeable effect on the number of enquiries or home page traffic.

The Personal Touch

Customer loyalty is an important aspect of all purchase behavior, even the purchase of stocks. As an intangible product, the purchase of stocks involves high levels of trust, and the building of personal relationships is a key factor in both attracting and retaining customers. Stock Exchanges

Figure 11.2 Search engine advertising (© Google 2013)

are personal networks as well as financial markets, and penetrating the relevant networks is a large part of a successful promotional strategy.

Online contact can seem both impersonal and intrusive, and it is important to mitigate these risks by including personal touches. We suggest adopting sales methods such as keeping a private note of relevant personal facts about key contacts, sending personal e-mails occasionally, seeking key contacts out at conferences and other events, sending Christmas cards and small corporate gifts, etc.

CHAPTER 12

Using New and Social Media

Social media is not easily defined. Definitions tend to focus either on the "community" aspect, the existence of "interactivity," or the availability of "user-generated content." In common speech, the term is used in a variety of ways, from a broad view which refers to almost everything on the Internet, to a middle view that regards social media as any Internet site which allows users to interact with other users and generate content, to a narrow view referring just to Facebook and similar highly flexible networking and friendship sites, with other interactive sites given dedicated categories such as blogs, wikis, file-sharing sites, and chat applications.

Social media has been defined as "any tool or service that uses the Internet to facilitate conversations" (Solis, 2011: 21). Kaplan and Haenlein (2010) define it as "a group of Internet-based applications that build on the ideological and technological foundations of Web 2.0, and that allow the creation and exchange of user-generated content." Social media has grown rapidly, with 96 percent of the online population now using one or more social media platforms (comScore MediaMetrix March 2012 Social Network U.S. category reach).

Despite the common use of the term *social media* as if social media were a family of platforms sharing common characteristics, there are an immense number of platforms which share very little in common other than use of the Internet. The goal of all platforms is to facilitate communication between people of common interests, but how this is achieved differs widely. Some platforms use distance to associate users, others allow users to search for each other, some are strictly based on preexisting social networks, and some are product or institution based. Platforms differ widely in the richness of communication (i.e., their use of images, audio,

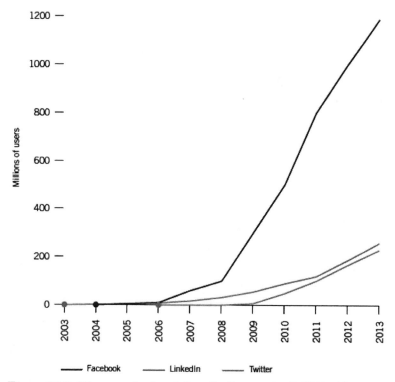

Figure 12.1 The growth of social media "mega-sites" (© Linklaters 2014)

video, and text), their degree of inclusivity vs. exclusivity, in frequency of messaging, and in the rules of communication. Some companies' proprietary messaging systems have evolved into quasi-social-media platforms, such as Amazon's system of product reviews, which allows reviewers to interact with each other, but most social media platforms are designed to be flexible and can be embedded in any web page.

Figure 12.1 shows the development of three of the largest social media platforms: Facebook, LinkedIn, and Twitter. The graph is taken from the report by Didizian and Cumbley, published by Linklaters in 2014: "Social media and the law: A handbook for U.K. companies."

Social media cannot be easily categorized, since each tool is unique and quickly evolving. There are some basic differences in purpose, as Figure 12.2 shows:

Purpose	Examples
Social networking	Facebook, LinkedIn, Tagged, Badoo, Myspace, Classmates, Hi5
Micro blogging	Twitter
Photo sharing	Flickr, Instagram, Pinterest
Video sharing	YouTube, Vimeo
Music sharing	SoundCloud
Film watching and review	Flixster
Forums and discussion boards	Yahoo! Groups, Google Groups
Social bookmarking	Delicious, Pinboard, Reddit, Digg
Blogs	MoneyBeat, Wonkblog
Online encyclopedias (wikis)	Wikipedia
News categorizing, sharing, and syndication platforms	RSS, Digg, Reddit
Product search and review sites	Yelp, foursquare
Dating and sex sites	Match, Grindr, Blendr
Messaging applications	WhatsApp, MSN Messenger, LINE
C2C product exchange	EBay

Figure 12.2 Basic social media categories

Kietzmann et al (2011) suggest that social media is composed of some or all of seven building blocks: identity, conversations, sharing, presence, relationships, reputation, and groups. Wikipedia, itself a social media site, lists 208 major social media platforms, not including online dating and defunct platforms.[1] Wikipedia lists 18 virtual communities that have more than 100 million active users[2] and 83 sites with more than 1 million active users.[3] Facebook is by far the leader in this scoreboard, with over a billion members. Looking at this list of 18 tools shows how diverse the range of social media is and how difficult defining social media is.

Argenti (2011) asserts that: "Embracing social media is no longer a strategic business option, but a necessity, and a huge opportunity." Social media, however, by its nature being hard to control brings real challenges

---

[1]http://en.wikipedia.org/wiki/List_of_social_networking_websites [accessed December 30, 2013]

[2]http://en.wikipedia.org/wiki/List_of_virtual_communities_with_more_than_100_million_users [accessed December 30, 2013]

[3]http://en.wikipedia.org/wiki/List_of_virtual_communities_with_more_than_1_million_users [accessed December 30, 2013]

for communication professionals, and this is especially true for investor relations (IR) professionals due to the potential financial and legal consequences of corporate disclosures. For investor relations officers (IROs), the additional challenges are the limited regulatory approval, the requirement to maintain traditional channels alongside new channels, and the twin hazards of negative sentiment and selective disclosure.

"Social media" is not a homogenous category, but a constantly growing and highly diverse range of tools. Corporate leaders need to figure out what social media can be and what they want to do with it.

The most commonly adopted uses of social media so far are:

- Feedback on products/services form customers (usually Facebook)
- Competitions and other public relations (PR) stunts (usually Facebook)
- Repository of corporate videos (YouTube) and
- Corporate responses to media stories (Twitter)

IR has limited use for social media for the following reasons: (1) IR does not generate a high volume of news, and investors and analysts would not welcome this; (2) social media is largely an "opt-in" technology, and so does not easily fit the requirement that all investor communication must be equally accessible to all; (3) stocks are not bought frequently by investors, but are long-term purchases; therefore, investors do not need regular stimulation to purchase; (4) IR typically does not have the resource to dedicate to generating a stream of verified and compliant (i.e., nonmaterial) news stories; (5) many social media platforms give users the ability to comment on messages, which can mean that corporate messaged can rapidly be "framed" in a negative way; (6) social media content is hard to store or reference.

Because of these factors, IR can best use social media by piggybacking on the company's social media output already generated by the corporate PR function. Ideally, options will be provided so that users can choose what kind of news feed they require. Investors who want constant social media news can opt into this by signing up for the category of "financial news."

Figure 12.3, which is taken from Business Insider, shows an estimate of the largest social networks in the world. Facebook and YouTube are the

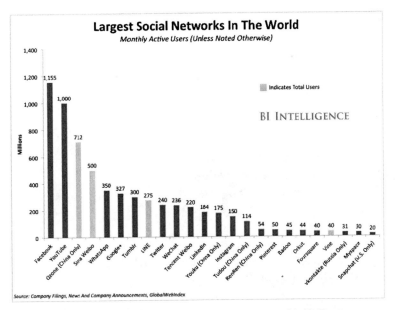

Figure 12.3 The largest social networks in the world (© Business Insider 2013)

current mega-sites, but the rapid pace of change within technology and consumer tastes means there is no guarantee this will last for long.

While the growth of public information has solved some long-standing problems of the financial markets, the deluge of public information (of varying quality and relevance) has introduced a range of new challenges.

The financial services sector uses social media little compared to other sectors, as demonstrated by research conducted in July 2009 by Altimeter/Wetpaint ENGAGEMENTdb in a study of the social media engagement of the top 100 brands. This is displayed in Figure 12.4.

Research in the United States by MHP Communications in 2011 (Sherman, 2011) indicated that investors are very slow in adopting social media tools, with Twitter only used by 35 percent of investors, YouTube used by 29 percent, and Facebook used by just 11 percent. LinkedIn was the social media tool of choice with a penetration of 96 percent, although a significant proportion of LinkedIn usage is likely to be job hunting rather than investment research.

A survey by Corbin Perception for the National Investor Relations Institute (NIRI) in June 2013 found that 72 percent of surveyed IR

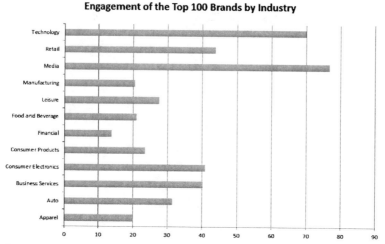

Figure 12.4 Social media use by industry (©Altimeter/Wetpaint ENGAGEMENTdb 2009)

professionals don't currently use social media for IR and less than half of them will consider doing so in the next 12 months. The same survey found that although most investors feel obliged to check the social media sites of the companies they analyze as part of their due diligence, 92 percent of investors consider the information gleaned from social media sites as either "somewhat unreliable" or "not at all reliable." Research in the United Kingdom by Furlong PR (Hay, 2010) found that the websites of 78 percent of the FTSE100 lacked basic social media functionality such as a blog and RSS feed.

Social Media Costs and Benefits

Social media brings serious costs and risks as well as benefits to corporations, and especially to heavily regulated areas of corporate life such as IR.

Social media by its nature is rapid, tends toward the trivial, fun, ephemeral, and gossipy, and is content rich (although this varies greatly with some services like Twitter being content poor). While some social media tools are private and person-to-person (such as WhatsApp), most communicate to a predefined group. Public access to this information varies. Twitter is public for instance, while to view Facebook posts requires membership of Facebook. Many social media are relationship based, and many users expect companies to actively engage in conversation with their customers. Investors expect more relevant and timely updates, increased transparency, and real time interaction and conversations with companies that are on social media. Investors would like to receive market and economic trends and commentary, new product information, company background, and product performance updates. Organizations usually insist on high degrees of control over their interactions with customers or the public, in order to reinforce their brand and market positioning and to avoid the hazards of making exaggerated claims about products or the risks of giving offense.

The anonymity and lack of editorial control mean that social media sites can be very angry places, with conversations getting very ugly. As well as the universal risks of fraud, hacking, identity theft, trolling, data theft, defamation, cyberbullying, and invasion of privacy, there are the risks of breaching regulations regarding selective disclosure. The costs include IT setup, training, management time producing and checking content, staff time lost through misuse of sites, and the time and cost of resolving problems. Three particular barriers to greater use of social media in IR are time and budget constraints, confusion over regulatory responsibilities, and concerns about the loss of control when interacting with social media platforms. IR, and investment more broadly, possesses a very risk-averse compliance structure and culture, which hampers the penetration of new tools.

Figure 12.5 shows the responses to the question on risk in the Grant Thornton survey of 2011:

What Is the Most Important Social Media Risk?

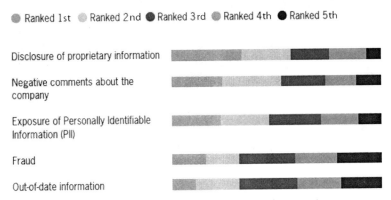

Figure 12.5 Social media risks (© Grant Thornton 2012)

Five Aspects of Social Media

We suggest that there are three essential aspects of social media for investors (1 to 3), one recommended aspect, (4) and one aspect that should be used with great caution (5)

1. **Social media policy formulation.** This is part of the disclosure policy mentioned below. In a survey by Katz and McIntosh (2013), three-quarters of company executives questioned said that their companies have no social media guidelines for employees.

2. **Social media monitoring.** Social media are not known for their coverage of financial news, but stories about the corporation, its products, or people may circulate on social media, and thus the monitoring of social media is an essential practice as an early warning of negative stories. It is essential to create company accounts on the major social media platforms such as Twitter, StockTwits, SeekingAlpha, etc. Establish alerts for social media and other online mentions of your company's stock symbol, brand names, key products, competition, key partners, and members of management and the board. For Twitter, download a desktop application such as TweetDeck or Hootsuite, which will make it easier to manage your search results. Make sure the IR team has a good link to the PR team member who monitors social media for consumer news, to get early warning of consumer issues that may develop into investor issues such as product-related problems, service failures, complaints about advertising, etc.

3. **Issue and opinion leader identification.** Careful monitoring of social media will enable identification of both issues and opinion leaders. Social media is dominated by a small proportion of users who generate content (perhaps just 1 percent), and a larger group (perhaps 10 percent) who comment on that created content. The remaining 90 percent of users are typically passive spectators. Identifying the sources of stories is an essential part of understanding how stories develop and how to counter them. Every organization is likely to have certain "issues" hard wired into its particular business model, but also additional issues will be generated by particular

media or public concerns of the moment. Informing management about issues at early stages is an essential part of developing an effective response, and so clear policies of escalation should be created.

4. **Social media linking.** This refers to the additional distribution of corporate news that has already been released via the recognized and official channels of regulatory news service (RNS) and corporate website. The social media content is purely incremental and supplements the comprehensive disclosure that was made prior to the social media distribution. The potential problem is that individuals can then comment on the news story using social media, which may involve criticism. The social media content must be distributed after the RNS and website content to ensure that disclosure is not selective. We suggest that social media content is uploaded a full hour after the RNS announcement (e.g., at 8 a.m. along with the e-mail to staff, if the RNS announcement was issued at 7 a.m.) to prevent any possibility of selective disclosure. Using social media to post links to the full announcement on the company home page is preferable to posting edited summaries on social media. This method allows for the beneficial advertising effect from social media, but eliminates the regulatory risk.

5. **Social media originated content.** This is of limited value for investor communications. The very aspects of social media that make it so valuable for consumers who are hunting for products or politicians who are trying to find out the public opinion of a proposed policy (i.e., its informality, personal and democratic nature, and the ability to speak in relative privacy to individuals, specified groups, and random strangers) make it unsuitable for disclosure of material corporate information. After monitoring social media discretely for a while, you will be able to decide whether it would be useful for your company to engage in particular social media channels or not. If a large proportion of your target audience uses a social media channel, then engaging in this channel must be considered. However, clear rules must be established for content creation and verification to prevent inaccurate or otherwise damaging content.

Selecting the Right Social Media

Social media show great variation in the following:

1. Penetration of the particular target audience that the company wishes to reach
2. Credibility of the site for corporate messages
3. Richness allowed in the message communicated
4. Access to the site, whether a personal profile must be created before access is granted or whether access is available for all
5. Ability to recall or edit messages
6. Ability to block negative comments
7. Ability to store messages in an easily searchable form

These are the factors that allow a company to select the right media for its investor communication.

Mobile Websites and Applications

Most FTSE100 companies now facilitate the use of their website on smartphones or tablets, either through the provision of a distinct URL that reformats the content to allow easier use on a device, or a dedicated downloadable application. The BASF plc mobile website is designed for smartphones and is pictured in Figure 12.6:

Investor Relations mobile web

BASF offers smartphone users an improved service with its new mobile website. Content is specifically tailored to the needs of mobile Internet users. Fast mobile access will provide answers to the most important questions about BASF.

Please benefit from the service of the BASF Investor Relations Team to the latest info, wherever you go.

We have set up the following topics for you:

- Information on the BASF share
- Stock Chart
- Investor Releases
- Links to the BASF Reports
- Calendar
- Detailed information on our Reporting and Annual Shareholders' Meeting
- Contact details
- Subscription of our IR newsletter

Figure 12.6 Example of an IR website adapted for smartphones (© BASF 2013)

Pirelli offer a "Corporate App" designed for iPads, which is accessible free via Apple's iTunes store.

Using Social Media for Disclosure

Regulators in the United States and United Kingdom have exhibited glacial speed in issuing guidance on the use of the Internet for corporate disclosure. The Financial Reporting Council in the United Kingdom has to date (Feb 2015) still issued no guidance on the acceptability of the Internet for disclosure. Even in the United States, the birthplace of the web, it wasn't until 2008 that the U.S. Securities and Exchange Commission (SEC) issued guidance on using the Internet to disclose. The 2008 guidance stated that *whether a company's web site is a recognised channel of distribution will depend on the steps that the company has taken to alert the market to its web site and its disclosure practices, as well as the use by investors and the market of the company's web site.* (SEC, 2008)

The United States' Financial Industry Regulatory Authority (FINRA) first issued guidance in January 2006, with the release of Notice 10-06. This generated lots of queries and FINRA-issued clarification with answers to 14 FAQs in August 2011 in Notice 11 to 39. FINRA neither encourages nor discourages the use of social media. The picture in the United States is complicated by the existence of state laws on the same matter; 11 states have so far passed legislation prohibiting employers from seeking access to personal social media accounts of employees, which might prevent companies in these states from complying with the FINRA guidance on employee supervision.

In April 2013, the SEC finally ruled that social media could be used to disclose financial results, following the case of Netflix Chief Executive Officer Reed Hastings, who on July 3, 2012, posted June's record monthly viewership result of 1 billion hours to the 200,000 followers on his personal Facebook page rather than in an SEC filing or news release.

Five months after the post, in December 2012, the SEC threatened Netflix and its CEO with enforcement action, with the issue of a "Wells Notice" to each of them, considering this as a potential selective release of material information and breach of "RegFD" (Regulation Fair Disclosure) and Section 13(a) of the U.S. Securities Exchange Act 1934. Four months after the threat, in April 2013, the SEC issued a statement which criticized Netflix noting that neither Hastings nor Netflix had previously used Hasting's personal Facebook page to distribute company information, and the SEC found that the company had not taken any steps to make the public aware that this could be used. The SEC, however, declined to state whether the information concerned was material and also declined to prosecute, instead using the opportunity to issue additional guidance on how companies should interpret RegFD[4] and the 2008 guidance in their use of social media. The 2013 update makes clear that the 2008 principle that states that the investing public should be alerted to the channels of distribution a company will use to disseminate material information applies with equal force to corporate disclosures made through social media channels.[5]

Given the lack of clarity in the United States and United Kingdom about what constitutes selective disclosure, particularly the absence of a definition of what constitutes "material" information, all actors (companies, investors, analysts, and journalists) would be wise to adopt a conservative stance and deploy the cautionary principle on disclosures, neither requesting nor providing nonpublic material information outside of the recognized methods of public disclosure. Publishing information on a narrowly defined communication vehicle such as Twitter and Facebook will not make that information "public" in the sense that all investors will have the information at the same time.

The main principle to follow is that since appropriate notice must be given to investors of the specific channels a company will use, the safest approach is that *all material investment information should be available via the IR corporate homepage.* An extra precautionary principle is that all new information must be e-mailed to everyone who has signed up to e-mail alerts; the link for which must again be available on the IR home page.

---

[4]Reg FD was issued by the SEC in August 2000 and requires that public companies communicate material information to investors on a broad, nonexclusive basis, in order to prevent favored analysts or investors obtaining extra information or early information. Reg FD is very conservative and a report on Form 8-K is the only method that categorically complies with it.

[5]www.sec.gov/News/PressRelease/Detail/PressRelease/1365171513574#.UsG9H_vuVHc

The social media posting should include a link to the full announcement on the company website so that all users are guided to the "one place."

If what Netflix did on July 2, 2012, was a material release (and the stock price uplift following the announcement might suggest that it was), then the company breached the 2008 guidance. They escaped a fine because the offense was mitigated by the absence of formal guidance, the wide coverage that the post received, the marginal nature of the information disclosed, and the long delay in the SEC's response. Firms that subsequently perform the same mistake may not be treated so leniently. The breach can be avoided by: (1) a clear understanding of what constitutes "material" information, (2) a clear procedure for handling material releases via the CFO or IRO, (3) use of a single place for all material information, and (4) prohibiting managers from releasing any nonpublic information about the firm on personal sites.

Any site that is not immediately available via a single click from the company homepage is not suitable as an exclusive location of corporate information. Any social networking site that requires a login (such as Facebook or LinkedIn) should not be used for disclosure, since the sites exclude nonmembers from access.

CHAPTER 13

The Future of Investor Relations

Seven main challenges can be identified for investor marketing; each of which presents good material for future research, whether academic or proprietary. These seven challenges are as follows: (1) The uncertain regulatory landscape of online investor relations (IR). Which social media channels have the greatest potential to satisfy the market's informational requirements without breaching compliance rules or creating reputation risks? How can corporations handle misinformation without being forced into increasing disclosure levels? Is two-way communication possible, legal, and desirable? At the same time, it may be incumbent upon the Financial Reporting Council, Securities and Exchange Commission, and other regulators to provide more precise guidance rather than waiting for companies to transgress before issuing clarification. (2) The uncertain future of sell-side analysts. How will analysts survive if all information is now publicly available? Who will pay for analyst research if all the information is already on the Internet? Is information alone enough, or does it require processing? Is there now too much information available, and might this increased disclosure be counterproductive? Do corporations need to provide a greater diversity of corporate information to match the diversity of investment styles? (3) The difficulty of justifying investing in relationships with analysts and investors in a climate of shortening investment horizons. How can IR prioritize the retention of existing shareholders and limit the revolving door of ownership that places so much strain on managerial time and restricts the development of long-term corporate strategy? (4) The reputational risks of social media tools and the difficulty of measuring the impact of social media on reputation and financial results. (5) The de-financialization of corporate value caused by the growth of intangibles. Intangible assets such as brands, knowledge, and reputation form an ever-increasing proportion of corporate value, but robust and consistent methods of measurement are lacking. The rather limited adoption of the "balanced scorecard" suggests that more research is required to provide managers and investors with metrics that they can rely on. (6) The internationalization of investment is a long-standing trend, which places additional pressures on IR. Remote investors may not be enthusiastic for contact and may use different approaches to valuation, corporate governance, communications, and financial reporting. Barriers of language and culture may make engagement a real challenge, and yet companies neglect overseas investors at their peril. (7) The final challenge to investor marketing is the reputational damage done to the entire investment industry by the financial crisis of 2007 to 2008, which undermined public confidence in the wealth generating ability of the stock market. This author believes that both the practice of investment and the art of marketing are activities that have a moral basis and generate social benefits. Investor marketing has a dual moral basis, as defending and advancing the social goals of investment in business and the social goals of the underlying businesses themselves. The economic and moral cases for the role of profit-seeking business in developed society have to be put regularly and persuasively in the "public square" as does the case for wide-scale share ownership and the role of investment, if the public's confidence in these essential institutions of modern capitalism is to be restored and the danger of still more burdensome regulation is to be averted.

If IR professionals are to maintain and increase their influence in the boardroom and guarantee the future of their profession, and the investment industry on which their profession depends, they will need to provide cogent and credible answers to challenges like these, challenges which will determine the relevance and influence of not just IR, but of the publically listed corporation for the next decade.

Conclusion

After establishing a marketing paradigm for the field of IR, this book reviewed research and practice on the marketing of corporate stock. It is clear that the benefits that the Internet offers in communicating with financial audiences are not yet being fully utilized by many companies, and encouragement from both regulators and information recipients would be helpful in accelerating this process. The uncertain regulatory framework is a major cause of the "digital conservatism" on display, and we would welcome regular updates of disclosure guidelines in this area.

Another area ripe for development is the conceptual analysis of IR. This field has been held back by the discreet nature of the relationship between investors and corporations and the prevalence of the Efficient Markets Hypothesis, which marginalizes the role of IR. We encourage academics to experiment with new research methods and new hypotheses in order to shed further light on this area, an area that can only grow in importance in the 21st century.

CHAPTER 14

Case Studies

Two short case studies are offered, both drawn from the United Kingdom over the last 10 years, to illustrate the importance of careful disclosure. The first case shows the consequence of a wrong judgment call on disclosure; the second case recounts a major fraud in which information was deliberately withheld from investors. The first case, while rather historic, is particularly valuable because it shows how easily serious errors in disclosure can be made inadvertently by well qualified and experienced executives.

Case 1—Delayed Disclosure at MyTravel plc (2002 to 2005)[1]

Between 1993 and 1999, Airtours plc grew at a rapid rate through acquisitions. Over this period turnover grew from £690m to £5.2bn. In November 1999, the chief financial officer (CFO), Tim Byrne, who had helped finance this program of growth, was appointed chief executive officer (CEO).

---

[1]This case study is based on the following sources:
- www.investegate.co.uk/article.aspx?id=200507140700098606O
- www.manchestereveningnews.co.uk/business/business-news/mytravel-fined-240000-1076813
- www.telegraph.co.uk/finance/2829725/Departure-lounge-for-MyTravel-chief.html
- http://news.bbc.co.uk/1/hi/business/4681739.stm
- www.ashurst.com/doc.aspx?id_Content=2028
- www.thisismoney.co.uk/money/news/article-1532624/FSA-confirms-probe-at-MyTravel.html
- www.theguardian.com/technology/2004/nov/27/business.travelnews

On Tuesday, September 11, 2001, four U.S. passenger airliners were hijacked by 19 al-Qaeda terrorists in order to be flown into buildings in suicide attacks. The airline industry, which had already been experiencing overcapacity, would be severely affected by the loss of passenger confidence in the months following this terrorist incident. Airtours plc rapid expansion over the previous decade and their complete reliance on holidaymakers left them particularly exposed to this sudden downturn in demand.

On November 27, 2001, Airtours plc announced record results for the 12 months to September, with a profit of £147.4m. Industry insiders, however, knew that Airtours plc was far from immune from the trauma that the airline industry was experiencing because of the challenges of declining demand and increased security regulations. The industry was poorly positioned to deal with falling demand due to fixed capacity, low margins, substantial exit costs, and a surplus of players. Investors became very sensitive to signs of weakness in the industry, as they speculated which airlines would be the first to collapse.

In February 2002, Byrne rebranded the company MyTravel plc, while retaining the Airtours name as a consumer brand. In May 2002, MyTravel plc issued a profit warning. This profit warning was apparently rescinded on July 23, 2002, when MyTravel announced that group trading across all divisions was in line with expectations. About eight days after this announcement, on or about 31st July, the results of a review of the accounting records and balance sheets of certain MyTravel U.K. business units were disclosed to management. The review had identified a number of balances from prior years that totaled £24.3m that would need to be written off as a charge against profits in the financial year to September 30, 2002. These were accounting or reconciliation errors that had occurred in a number of years prior to 2002. The balances represented an inadvertent cumulative overstatement of the profits for FY01 and previous years, and it was agreed that they should be written off immediately and charged to the 2002 accounts.

The CFO (David Jardine) and CEO (Tim Byrne, who was himself a qualified accountant and had formerly been CFO) chose not to inform shareholders of the loss, believing that exceptional gains would offset the one-off cost. Byrne believed that the prior-year balances had been reflected in existing profit forecasts, that the overall profit target would be met and that because of this no announcement was necessary, since the prior-year adjustments merely represented a change in the timing of profits, not the overall level of profit. The board as a whole was not informed of the balances, and no external advice was solicited.

Following disagreements with management, the company's auditors, Arthur Andersen, were dismissed and Deloitte and Touche appointed. On 30th September the company issued a second profit warning. Following shareholder pressure, Tim Byrne was ousted as CEO on 8th October. The company then issued a third profit warning on 17th October after which shares fell further to 18pence, valuing the company at just £89m. Earlier that year the shares had been worth £2.84.

Peter McHugh (CEO of the Group's North American operations) was appointed as Chief Executive of MyTravel plc on October 17, 2002.

On 12th November, the Financial Services Authority (FSA) announced that it was proceeding with a preliminary investigation into MyTravel's disclosures concerning the timing of its September profit warning.

On 28th November, the prior-year exposures were finally announced to the market, as part of the full year results announcement.

The performance of MyTravel continued to worsen, and in December 2004 MyTravel agreed a £800m debt-for-equity swap that saw its debtors take ownership of 94 percent of the company's shares, while shareholders suffered a 30 for 1 share swap and retained just 4 percent with bondholders receiving the balance of 2 percent.

After a lengthy investigation, the FSA fined MyTravel on November 4, 2004. MyTravel immediately appealed to the Financial Services and Markets Tribunal. Finally on July 14, 2005, the FSA announced that a settlement had been reached and that MyTravel Group plc had accepted the fine of £240,000 and withdrawn its planned appeal. MyTravel had breached the Listing Rules in July 2002 by failing to update the market following a change in its own expectation as to its performance for the financial year ended on September 30, 2002. There had been a breach of Listing Rule 9.2(c) which obliged companies to make an announcement of information concerning a change in the company's expectations as to its performance which, if made public, would be likely to lead to a substantial movement in its share price. The FSA concluded that there had been a change in the expected source, composition, and timing of the company's profits, and that where such information, if made public, might lead to a substantial movement in its share price it must be announced. Although the officers of the company had this information around July 31, 2002, the firm did not announce this information until November 28, 2002. By failing to notify a Regulatory Information Service without delay, MyTravel contravened Listing Rule 9.2(c).

No individuals were fined. The FSA regarded the difficult market situation that prevailed at the time of the company's nondisclosure as an aggravating matter since investors would be particularly keen for performance updates. When the final settlement was announced, the managing director of the authority's wholesale business division, Hector Sants, said: *The need to inform the market was especially relevant in MyTravel's case, where the prevailing business environment was challenging and any announcement in relation to accounting issues would have come as an unwelcome surprise to investors.*

The FSA put particular emphasis on the situation of investor nervousness that existed within the travel sector generally but which applied to MyTravel in particular, given the announcements already made by it earlier in 2002. Underlying the decision in this case is the concept that it is not for the company management to conclude that a loss, in this case a large write off, will be compensated by gains elsewhere and therefore no announcement is necessary. The market must be given the opportunity to assess the information itself. MyTravel's failure to seek independent advice on the issue was a further aggravating factor which contributed to the calculation of the financial penalty.

A final noteworthy point is the position of the individual directors concerned, the former group finance director, and chief executive. The FSA accepted that their error was accidental and took no personal action against them.

Case 2—Misleading Disclosures at Cattles plc (2007 to 2012)[2]

Cattles was founded in Hull 1927 and listed on the London Stock Exchange in 1963. Cattles plc was a leading lender to the "subprime" market, lending to customers who had poor credit histories who would not receive credit from high street banks. The loans were unsecured and carried very high levels of interest. In 1994 Cattles plc purchased Welcome Financial Services. By 2007 Welcome Financial Services provided 90 percent of the revenue of Cattles plc.

In 2007, Cattles plc published an Annual Report which subsequently was shown to contain highly misleading statements of arrears, impairment, and profit. The arrears on Welcome Financial Services loan book of £3 billion was stated as £0.9 billion rather than the £1.5 billion, which would have been the figure if accounting standards had been correctly applied. A pretax profit of £165m was declared, when later calculations showed that Cattles actually suffered a pretax loss of £96.5 million for the year.

As the recession in the United Kingdom deepened, the financial position of Cattles plc worsened as more and more of its customers defaulted. Welcome had started to understate the extent of its bad debts by deliberately deferring loans without the knowledge of the customer so that loans would not be regarded as impaired as they should have been when they were 120 days late. Welcome was deliberately understating the proportion of bad debt it held, knowing that the ratio to bad debt to total debt was a key measure of financial performance used by investors.

In April 2008, Cattles plc, desperately short of cash, issued a rights issue prospectus to potential investors which included the misleading

---

[2]This case study is based on the following sources:
- www.ccrmagazine.com/index.php?option=com_content&task=view&id=6646&Itemid=99999999
- www.cattles.co.uk/about-us/company-history
- www.theguardian.com/business/2009/mar/10/loans-cattles-directors-covenants
- www.frc.org.uk/Our-Work/Publications/Professional-Discipline/Tribunal-Report-Peter-Miller-File.pdf

figures from the Annual Report. The rights issue was fully subscribed at £1.28 per share and raised £200 million.

In January 2009, the company announced the loss of 1,000 jobs. On March 10, 2009, the company issued its third profits warning in three weeks, and suspended three directors of the Welcome Financial Services subsidiary—James Corr (Finance Director), Ian Cummine (Chief Operating Officer), and Adrian Cummings (Compliance and Risk Director)—pending an investigation by Deloitte into accounting irregularities. By the end of the day the shares were worth 1.8pence, they had been 195pence 12 months earlier. In April 2009 trading in Cattles shares was suspended pending the publication of its report and accounts for the year ended on December 31, 2008. In July 2009, the above three directors were dismissed without compensation, and the Chairman Norman Broadhurst and CEO David Postings chose to leave the group. In December 2009, Cattles announced that its shares "are likely to have little or no value."

Cattles was acquired by Bovess Limited in February 2011. On March 2, 2011, Cattles announced a scheme of arrangement under which its shareholders would receive only 1p for each share.

On March 28, 2012, the FSA issued a final notice. James Corr, Cattles' finance director, was fined £400,000, and Peter Miller, Welcome's finance director, was fined £200,000, and both had been banned from performing any functions in relation to any FSA-regulated activities. The FSA also banned John Blake, Welcome's managing director, and fined him £100,000. All three fines were reduced on account of the directors' current personal financial circumstances. In 2013, Miller was expelled by the Financial Reporting Council from the Institute of Chartered Accountants for England and Wales for his role in the publication of the 2007 Annual Report and 2008 rights issue prospectus, both of which contained materially misleading information designed to create a false market in shares.

Cattles had breached the Listing Principles by failing to act with integrity toward its shareholders and potential shareholders, and failing to communicate information in such a way as to avoid the creation or continuation of a false market. Welcome breached Principle three of the FSA Principles for Businesses by failing to take reasonable care to organize and control its affairs responsibly and effectively, with adequate risk management systems. Both firms engaged in market abuse by disseminating the inaccurate information. Corr and Miller were personally responsible for the breaches by the companies of which they were directors and also committed market abuse.

The FSA publicly censured Cattles and Welcome, and stated that it would have imposed substantial financial penalties had it not been for the weak financial position of the firms. The firms cooperated fully with the FSA's investigation.

Tracey McDermott, the FSA's acting director of enforcement and financial crime, made this statement following the outcome of the investigation:

> The consequences for shareholders of the misleading statements issued by Cattles and Welcome have been devastating. These directors failed to act with integrity in discharging their responsibilities. They failed in their obligations to shareholders, the wider market and the regulator. In order for markets to function properly, information given to investors must be accurate. Directors of listed companies must act with integrity and exercise appropriate diligence when making disclosures to the market. They should note the personal consequences for those who fail to meet our requirements.

References

ACCA. 2013. *Understanding Investors: Directions for Corporate Reporting.* Glasgow, Scotland: Association of Chartered Certified Accountants.

Agarwal, V., X. A. Bellotti, and R.J. Taffler. 2009. *The Value Relevance of Effective Investor Relations.* Working paper version 6. London, England: Middlesex University Business School.

Argenti, P. 2011. Digital strategies for powerful corporate *communications. The European Financial Review,* February – March.

Berle, A. A., and G. C. Means. 1968. *The Modern Corporation and Private Property.* 2nd ed. New York, NY: Harcourt, Brace & World.

Bollen, L., H. Hassink, and G. Bozic. 2006. "Measuring and explaining the quality of Internet investor relations activities: A multinational empirical analysis." *International Journal of Accounting Information Systems* 7 (4), pp. 273–289.

Bollen, L. H. Fall, 2008. "Best Practices in Managing Investor Relations Websites: Directions for Future Research." *Journal of Information Systems* 22 (2), pp. 171–194.

Bonson, E., and F. Flores. 2011. "Social media and corporate dialogue: the response of global financial institutions." *Online Information Review* 35 (1), pp. 34–49.

Brennan, M. J., and C. Tamaronski. 2000. "Investor Relations, Liquidity and Stock Prices." *Journal of Applied Corporate Finance* 12 (4), pp. 26–37.

Brennan, N., and S. Kelly. August, 2000. "Use of the internet by Irish companies for investor relations purposes." *Accountancy Ireland,* pp. 23–25.

Bushee, B. J., and G. S. Miller. August, 2007. "Investor Relations, Firm Visibility, and Investor Following." *Working Paper.* Philadelphia, PA: *Wharton School.*

Buttle, F. 1986. *Hotel and Food Service Marketing: A Managerial Approach,* London, England: Cassell.

Cadbury, A. 1992. *Report of the Committee on the Financial Aspects of Corporate Governance.* London: Gee & Co. Ltd.

Citigate Dewe Rogerson. 2014. *Investor Relations Survey: Increasing returns on IR investment.* Citigate Dewe Rogerson.

Coe, J. M. 2004. *The Fundamentals of Business to Business Sales and Marketing.* New York, NY: McGraw Hill.

Craven, B. M., and C. L. Marston. 1999. "Financial reporting on the Internet by leading UK companies." *European Accounting Review* 8 (2), pp. 321–334.

Deller, D., M. Stubenrath, and C. Weber. 1999. "A survey on the use of the Internet for investor relations in the USA, the UK and Germany." *European Accounting Review* 8 (2), pp. 351–364.

Didizian, M. and R. Cumbley, 2014. *Social Media and The Law: A Handbook for UK Companies.* London: Linklaters LLP.

Drucker, P. F. 1954. *The Practice of Management.* New York, NY: Harper & Brothers.

Ellis, C. D. 1985. "How to manage investor relations", *Financial Analysts Journal* 41, pp. 34–41.

Falkow, S. 2010. "Engagement – the new ROI? [weblog entry]," The Proactive Report: Anticipating PR Trends Online. www.proactivereport.com

Fama, E. F. 1965a. "The behavior of stock market prices." *Journal of Business* 38 (January), pp. 34–105.

Fama, E. F. 1965b. *Random Walks in Stock Market Prices.* Selected Papers, no. 16, Chicago, IL: University of Chicago.

Fama, E. F. 1980. Agency Problems and the Theory of the Firm, *The Journal of Political Economy 88*, (2) pp. 288-307.

Francis, J., J. D. Hanna, and D. R Philbrick. 1997. "Management Communications with Security Analysts." *Journal of Accounting & Economics* 24, pp. 363–394.

FRC. 2013. *Audit Quality Thematic Review.* London, England: Financial Reporting Council.

Gaved, M. 1997. "Closing the Communications Gap: Disclosure and Institutional Shareholders". London: The Institute of Chartered Accountants in England & Wales.

Golding, T. 2003. *The City: Inside the Great Expectation Machine.* Harlow, England: Prentice – Hall.

Gowthorpe, C. 2004. "Asymmetrical dialogue? Corporate financial reporting via the Internet." *Corporate Communications: An International Journal* 9 (4), pp. 283–293.

Groysberg, B., and P. M. Healy. 2013. *Wall Street Research: Past, Present and Future.* Stanford, California: Stanford University Press.

Groysberg, B., P. M. Healy, and D. Maber. 2011. "What drives sell-side analyst compensation at high-status investment banks?" *Journal of Accounting Research 49* (4), pp. 969–1000.

Gruner, R. H. 2002. "Corporate disclosure: the key to restoring investor confidence". *Strategic Investor Relations* 2(2), pp. 12–15.

Hay, P. 18 June 2010. "Corporates 'must act' on social media". *PR Week UK*, p. 12.

Hirschmann, A. O. 1970. *Exit, Voice & Loyalty: Responses to Decline in Firms, Organizations and States.* Cambridge, Mass: Harvard University Press.

Hobor, N. 1997. "Investor Relations for Shareholder Value" In *The Handbook of Strategic Public Relations and Integrated Public Relations*, ed. Clarke L. Caywood. New York, NY: McGraw-Hill.

Holland, J. 1998. "Private Voluntary Disclosure, Financial Intermediation and Market Efficiency." *Journal of Business Finance and Accounting* 25 (1), pp. 29–66.

Houston, J. 1986. "The Marketing Concept: What It Is and What It Is Not." *Journal of Marketing* 50 (2), pp. 81–87.

Houston, J. 2013. *Online Investor Communications: A Survival Guide.* Birmingham, England: Jones and Palmer.

Hussey, R., J. Gulliford, and A. Lymer. 1998. *Corporate Communication: Financial Reporting on the Internet.* London, England: Deloitte Touche Tohmatsu.

Jensen, M., & Meckling, W. 1976. "Theory of the firm: Managerial Behavior, Agency Costs and Ownership Structure." *Journal of Financial Economics 3*, pp. 305–360.

Junkus, J.C., and T.C. Berry. 2010. "The Demographic Profile of Socially Responsible Investors." *Managerial Finance* 36 (6), pp. 474–481.

Kaplan A. M., and M. Haenlein. 2010. "Users of the world, unite! The challenges and opportunities of social media." *Business Horizons* 53 (1), p. 61.

Katz, D. A. and L. A. McIntosh. 2013. "Corporate Governance Update: The Board, Social Media and Regulation FD." *New York Law Journal* March 28, 2013.

Keith, R. J. January, 1960. "The Marketing Revolution." *Journal of Marketing* 24, pp. 35–38.

Kietzmann, J H., et al. 2011. "Social media? Get serious! Understanding the functional building blocks of social media." *Business Horizons* 54 (3), pp. 241–251.

Kleinfield, N. R. 1985. "The Many Faces of the Wall Street Analyst." *New York Times*, 27th October 1985.

Kotler, P., and S. J. Levy. January, 1969. "Broadening the Concept of Marketing." *The Journal of Marketing* 33, pp. 10–15.

Kotler, P., and S. J. Levy. Winter, 1969. "Beyond Marketing: The Furthering Concept." *California Management Review* 12, pp. 67–73.

Kotler, P. and S. J. Levy. November-December. 1971. "Demarketing, Yes, Demarketing." *Harvard Business Review* 49, pp. 71–80.

Kotler, P. April, 1972. "A Generic Concept of Marketing." *The Journal of Marketing* 36 (2), pp. 46–54.

Kotler, P. 1973. "Defining the Limits of Marketing", *1972 Fall Conference Proceedings of the American Marketing Association* pp. 48–56.

Kotler, P., and S. J. Levy. January, 1973. "Buying is Marketing Too!" *The Journal of Marketing,* 37 (1), pp. 54–59.

Kotler, P. October, 1973. "The Major Tasks of Marketing Management." *The Journal of Marketing* 37 (4), pp. 42–49.

Kotler, P. and Murray, M. September-October, 1975. "Third Sector Management – The Role of Marketing." *Public Administration Review* 35 (5), pp. 467–472.

Kotler, P., and W. Mindak. October, 1978. "Marketing and Public Relations." *The Journal of Marketing* 42 (4), pp. 13–20.

Kotler, P., and K. Keller. 2011. *Marketing Management.* 14th ed. Upper Saddle River, NJ: Pearson.

Kotler, P. and G. Zaltman. 1971. "Social Marketing: An Approach to Planned Social Change." *Journal of Marketing* 35 (July), pp. 3–12.

Krapfel, R. E. 1982, "Marketing by Mandate." *Journal of Marketing* 46 (Summer), pp. 79–85.

Lang, M. H., and R. J. Lundholm. 1996. "Corporate Disclosure Policy and Analyst Behaviour." *The Accounting Review* 71 (4), pp. 215–254.

Lee, T. A. and D. P Tweedie. 1977. *The Private Shareholder and the Corporate Report*, London, England: ICAEW.

Lesly, P. 1971. *Lesly's Public Relations Handbook.* New York, NY: Prentice-Hall.

Lev, B. Summer. 1992. "Information Disclosure Strategy." *California Management Review* pp. 9–32.

Lev, B. and P. Zarowin. 1999. "The Boundaries of Financial Reporting and How to Extend Them." *Journal of Accounting Research* 37 (2) (Autumn) pp. 353–385.

Lymer, A. and A. Tallberg. April, 1997. *Corporate reporting and the Internet – a survey and commentary on the use of the world wide web in corporate reporting in the UK and Finland.* Paper presented at the 20th Annual Congress of the European Accounting Association, Graz, Austria.

Maltby, J. 1998. "UK joint stock companies legislation 1844-1900: accounting publicity and 'mercantile caution.'" *Accounting History* 3 (9).

May, G. 1932. "The Accountant and the Investor" A lecture delivered in 1932 at the William A. Vawter Foundation of Business Ethics, Northwestern University School of Commerce, New York.

McKee, Thomas.E. 2005. Earnings Management: An Executive Perspective, New York, NY: South-Western.

McKenna, R. January–February, 1991. "Marketing is everything." *Harvard Business Review* 69, pp. 65–79.

Mintzberg, H. 1987. "Five Ps for Strategy." *California Management Review* 30 (1) pp. 11–24.

Nielsen, C., and P. N. Bukh. 2011. *Investor Relations: Communicating Strategy from a Business Model Perspective.* Working Paper Series, no 1. Aalborg, Denmark: Aalborg University Department of Business and Management.

NIRI. 2003. Definition of Investor Relations, Adopted by the Board of Directors, National Investor Relations Institute, March 2003 www.niri.org/about/mission.cfm

Peters, T. and R. Waterman. 1982. *In Search of Excellence.*, New York, NY: Harper & Row.

Porter, M. 1980. *Corporate Strategy.* New York, NY: Free Press.

Rentz, K. C. 1992. "The value of narrative in business writing." *The Journal of Business and Technical Communication* 6, pp. 293–315.

Roberts, J., et al. 2011. "In the Mirror of the Market: the Disciplinary Effects of Company/Fund Manager Meetings", Working Paper No. 290, Cambridge: *ESRC Centre for Business Research*, Judge Institute of Management, University of Cambridge.

SEC. August 7, 2008. *Commission Guidance on the use of Company Web Sites* (Release 34-58288). Washington, DC: Securities and Exchange Commission.

SEC. April 2, 2013. *Report of Investigation: Netflix, Inc., and Reed Hastings* (Release 69279). Washington, DC: Securities and Exchange Commission.

Sherman, E. Autumn. 2011. "Asset managers are not social butterflies." *IR Magazine*.

Smith, T. 1992. *Accounting for Growth: Stripping the Camouflage from Company Accounts*. London, England: Century Business.

Sollis, B. 2011. *Engage! The Complete Guide for Brands and Businesses to Build, Cultivate, and Measure Success in the New Web*. Hoboken, NJ: Wiley.

Solomon, D. and E. Soltes. 2013. *What Are We Meeting For? The Consequences of Private Meetings with Investors*, Working Paper, January, Harvard Business School.

Valentine, D. R. September, 2013. *Extending the concept of marketing . . . further still*. Liverpool, England: British Academy of Management Conference.

Webster Jr., F. E. 1994. *Market-driven Management*. Hoboken, NJ: Wiley.

Further Reading

Bragg, S. 2010. *Running an Effective Investor Relations Department: A Comprehensive Guide*. 6th ed. Hoboken, NJ: Wiley.

Guimard, A. 2013. *Investor Relations: Principles and International Best Practices in Financial Communications*. 2nd ed. Basingstoke, England: Palgrave MacMillan.

Lev, B. 2012. *Winning Investors Over: Surprising Truths about Honesty, Earnings Guidance, and Other Ways to Boost Your Stock Price*. Boston, MA: Harvard Business Review Press.

Westbrook, I. 2014. *Strategic Financial and Investor Communication: The Stock Price Story*. London, England: Routledge.

About the Author

Daniel Valentine, MCIPR, MCIM, FRSA, was previously a senior Investor Relations Officer for companies listed on the FTSE250 and FTSE100. He is currently Director of Communications for one of the UK's best known organisations, Visiting Professor of Strategic Management at a leading European business school, and Research Director of Oxford University's "UK Investor Engagement Survey", an annual measure of best practice in financial communications.

Daniel is a recognised expert in investor marketing and public relations and has spoken at conferences in Europe, the Middle East, Africa and Asia. Through consulting, training and speaking, Daniel has helped organizations large and small all over the world. He has been interviewed on countless news programmes and is regularly contacted for comment by leading news agencies.

A graduate of Oxford University, the University of St Andrews and King's College London, Daniel served with the reserve forces in the Royal Corps of Signals, the combat arm that provides the communications throughout the command system of the British Army. Daniel is a member of the Oxford & Cambridge, East India, and Victory Service Clubs.

Daniel welcomes comments on this book, which can be sent to daniel.valentine@hertford.ox.ac.uk or daniel@daniel-valentine.com.

Index

OTHER TITLES IN OUR FINANCE AND FINANCIAL MANAGEMENT COLLECTION

John A. Doukas, Old Dominion University, Editor

- *Recovering from the Global Financial Crisis: Achieving Financial Stability in Times of Uncertainty* by Marianne Ojo
- *Introduction to Foreign Exchange Rates* by Thomas J. O'Brien
- *Applied International Finance: Managing Foreign Exchange Risk and International Capital Budgeting* by Thomas J. O'Brien
- *Venture Capital in Asia: Investing in Emerging Countries* by William Scheela
- *Global Mergers and Acquisitions: Combining Companies Across Borders* by Abdol S. Soofi and Yuqin Zhang
- *Essentials of Retirement Planning: A Holistic Review of Personal Retirement Planning Issues and Employer-Sponsored Plans* by Eric J. Robbins
- *The Fundamentals of Financial Statement Analysis as Applied to the Coca-Cola Company* by Carl B. McGowan, Jr., John C. Gardner, and Susan E. Moeller
- *Corporate Valuation Using the Free Cash Flow Method Applied to Coca-Cola* by Carl B McGowan, Jr.
- *Capital Budgeting* by Sandeep Goel

Announcing the Business Expert Press Digital Library

Concise e-books business students need for classroom and research

This book can also be purchased in an e-book collection by your library as

- a one-time purchase,
- that is owned forever,
- allows for simultaneous readers,
- has no restrictions on printing, and
- can be downloaded as PDFs from within the library community.

Our digital library collections are a great solution to beat the rising cost of textbooks. E-books can be loaded into their course management systems or onto students' e-book readers.
The **Business Expert Press** digital libraries are very affordable, with no obligation to buy in future years. For more information, please visit www.businessexpertpress.com/librarians. To set up a trial in the United States, please email **sales@businessexpertpress.com**.

CPSIA information can be obtained
at www.ICGtesting.com
Printed in the USA
FFOW01n0225050515
13042FF

9 781631 571404